D0111374

INTERPERSONAL PEACEMAKING: CONFRONTATIONS AND THIRD-PARTY CONSULTATION

INTERPERSONAL PEACEMAKING: CONFRONTATIONS AND THIRD-PARTY CONSULTATION

RICHARD E. WALTON

Graduate School of Business, Harvard University

ADDISON-WESLEY PUBLISHING COMPANY

Reading, Massachusetts · Menlo Park, California

London · Amsterdam · Don Mills, Ontario · Sydney

This book is in the Addison-Wesley series:

ORGANIZATION DEVELOPMENT

Editors
Edgar Schein
Warren Bennis
Richard Beckhard

TO SHARON
*partner in
love and life*

ISBN 0-201-08435-X
NOPQRSTUVW-DO-79

FOREWORD

The purpose of this common foreword to all the volumes of the Addison-Wesley Series on Organization Development is twofold: (1) to give the reader some idea as to the origin and purpose of the series; and (2) to guide the reader through the content of the different books.

The series came to be because we felt there was a growing theory and practice of something called "organization development," but most students, colleagues, and managers knew relatively little about it. Many of us are highly active as OD consultants, but little has been written about what we do when we are with a client or what our underlying theory of consultation is. We were also acutely aware of the fact that, though there are common assumptions shared by most practitioners of OD, there are great individual variations in the strategies and tactics employed by different consultants. The field is still emerging and new methods are constantly being invented. It seemed appropriate, therefore, not to try to write a single text, but to give several of the foremost theorist-practitioners a chance to explain their own view of OD and their own style of working with client systems.

The authors of this series of six books represent a variety of points of view, but they do not exhaust the major approaches currently in use in OD. There are some obvious names missing—Argyris, Tannenbaum, Ferguson, Bradford, Davis, Burke—to name just a few. We hope in future volumes of the series to get these men and others to write about their theory and practice.

The six books of this series can be described as follows: Bennis presents a very broad overview of the history and present practice of OD. How and why did it come about, what is it, and what are some of the major unresolved issues in OD? The Beckhard volume is a systematic attempt to describe the various strategies and tactics employed in different kinds of OD efforts. Beckhard goes beyond his own approach and tries to build a general framework within which most OD programs can be located. The Beckhard and Bennis volumes together give the reader an excellent overview of the field.

The two volumes by Blake and Mouton and by Lawrence and Lorsch are somewhat more personalized statements of their particular views of how organizations function, how organizational excellence is to be judged, and how an OD effort can contribute to the achievement of such excellence. Both books are focused on total organization systems and attempt to show how intervention in organizations leads to constructive change and development.

The volumes by Walton and Schein are written at a more specific level. They highlight some of the day-to-day activities of the consultant as he works with a client system in the context of an OD program. Both deal with the process of the consultation itself. In the Walton book the focus is on the process by which the consultant uses himself to aid in the resolution of conflict. In the Schein book the idea of "process consultation" is introduced and explained in detail. The kinds of organizational processes which are described in these last two volumes lie at the heart of OD efforts, but the focus of the books is on the moment-to-moment behavior of the consultant rather than the overall design of the OD program.

The six books were written independently with only broad guidelines and minimum coordination by the editors. It was our hope and intention to get six very personal and unique statements, rather than a closely integrated set of "chapters." We feel that the amount of overlap is minimal, and that the books in fact complement each other very well in being written at different levels of generality. We hope that the reader will sense that the field of OD is converging toward common theories and practices, but that we are a long way from being able to produce a definitive "text" on the subject.

March 1969   Edgar H. Schein
                                                Richard Beckhard
                                                Warren G. Bennis

PREFACE

This is the era of confrontations. Almost daily we witness a newsworthy confrontation—between races, between the poor and the establishment, between students and university administrators, between the younger and older generations, and so on. The trend is also felt inside organizations. Managers are becoming more inclined to acknowledge and confront rather than smooth over their differences.

We increasingly understand that psychological and social energy is tied up in suppressing conflict, that conflicts not confronted may be played out in indirect and destructive ways, and that the differences that underlie interpersonal conflict often represent diversity or complementarity of significant potential value to the organization. An interpersonal or organizational system that can acknowledge and effectively confront its internal conflicts has a greater capacity to innovate and adapt.

Unfortunately, our knowledge about and skill in confrontation methods lags our increasing preference or tolerance for this approach to conflict. As a result, direct confrontations between participants frequently are ineffective or inappropriate. The confrontation can escalate and polarize a conflict, just as it can serve as the first step toward resolution or better control. Thus, the question becomes: how can we minimize the risks and enhance the effectiveness of direct confrontation and other modes of conflict management?

Third-party consultation (by organizational members or outside consultants) can in many ways help increase the likelihood of constructive outcomes from conflict. For example, the third-party consultant may work to ensure mutual motivation on the part of principals, to create parity in their situational power, to synchronize their negative and positive moves, to provide the social support and process expertise that enhance openness. Additionally, the third party may perform a translation function and act to adjust the tension to optimum levels.

While the potential exists, in practice third-party roles in the organizational setting have not been recognized and legitimated as they have been in other settings such as labor mediation services, the UN Secretariat and its peace-keeping units, and marital counseling. This book seeks to accelerate the emergence of third-party consultation as an integral part of organizational development programs. Also, the insight gained by analyzing the constructive influences of third parties can be used by conflict principals themselves who want to break out of the conflict pattern.

More than intellectual understanding will be required, however. The effective use of the knowledge contained in this book depends upon a personal capacity to be open and confronting in human encounters when the situation calls for it. This is the quality that our child-rearing and other socialization processes have promoted in some, but not most, people. Many organizational development programs in business, government, and education, however, are currently operating to develop the interpersonal skills and to create the interpersonal climate conducive to the type of conflict resolution methodology treated here.

Research for this volume was supported by the Advanced Research Projects Agency of the Department of Defense and was monitored by the Air Force Office of Scientific Research under Contract No. F44620-69-C-0040. Administrative support was provided by the Division of Research, Harvard Graduate School of Business Administration. Needless to say I greatly appreciate the support of these institutions.

I am indebted to the principals in the several conflict episodes reported here—in which I participated as the third-party consultant—for they subsequently assisted and encouraged me to first document, and then derive the lessons from, these practical ventures in conflict resolution.

I am grateful for the reactions and advice of colleagues who read the manuscript at various stages, including Peter Block, Samuel Culbert, Edgar Schein, John Sherwood, and Leonard Solomon. Also, my thanks to Frida Pomerantz who commented helpfully on the manuscript and managed it through its various drafts.

Boston, Massachusetts   R.E.W.
January 1969

CONTENTS

1

INTRODUCTION

This book concerns the theory and practice of third parties who would help two members of an organization manage their interpersonal conflict. It presents a model for diagnosing recurrent conflict between two persons. Then on the basis of our understanding of the dynamics of interpersonal-conflict episodes, we derive a number of strategic functions which a third party can perform to facilitate a constructive confrontation of the conflict. Having specified the potential third-party functions, we analyze the many tactical opportunities available to third parties and the tactical choices which must be made in performing third-party functions. Finally, in view of the functions he must perform and the tactical interventions he must execute, we postulate the optimum personal and positional attributes for the third party. The interpersonal peacemakers we contemplate include behavioral-science consultants but definitely are not confined to this class of professionals.

This volume includes three detailed case studies from which are induced many of the concepts, models, and propositions about interpersonal conflict and third-party functions, and from which are drawn illustrative third-party interventions. However, other propositions about the functions of third parties are deduced from the literature on psychological processes and interpersonal conflict.

INTERPERSONAL CONFLICT IN ORGANIZATIONS[1]

Although we believe that the theory and practice spelled out here has more general applicability, the book is directly focused on "interpersonal conflict in organizational contexts," such as differences between fellow members of a governing committee, heads of interrelated departments, a manager and his boss. Interpersonal conflict is defined broadly to include both (a) interpersonal disagreements over substantive issues, such as differences over organizational structures, policies, and practices, and (b) interpersonal antagonisms, that is, the more personal and emotional differences which arise between interdependent human beings.

Interdependence takes a variety of forms in organizations. One manager depends upon another for a technical service, for information or advice, for timely advancement of material in the work-flow process. One's behavior is controlled by the actions of another person or group just as one's performance is measured and evaluated by another. Substantial proportions of one's organizational life are spent in the presence of particular other persons.

The innumerable interdependencies inherent in organizations make interpersonal conflicts inevitable. Even if it were thought to be desirable, it would not be possible to create organizations free from interpersonal conflicts. But one can develop capacities within or available to organizations that make it possible to resolve more of these interpersonal conflicts and lessen the costs of those which cannot readily be resolved.

In order to improve the capacities of organizations to deal with

---

[1] In focusing on this area, the book contributes another dimension to a limited but significant existing literature on third parties. For example, the activities of the labor mediator have been reported by Ann Douglas in *Industrial Peacemaking*, New York: Columbia University Press, 1962. The processes of international mediation have been analyzed and illustrated by Oran Young in *The Intermediaries: Third Parties in International Crises*, Princeton: Princeton University Press, 1967. The processes of conjoint family therapy have been articulated by Virginia Satir in *Conjoint Family Therapy*, Palo Alto: Science and Behavior Books, Incorporated, 1964.

conflict, one must take into account several personal and organizational tendencies which typically operate to limit relatively direct approaches to conflict management.

Inhibitions are a factor. To express anger, resentment, or envy toward another member of a work organization is typically considered bad manners or immature. We usually are taught to be ashamed of those feelings and in any event, not to express them. In my consulting and research experience, members of organizations nevertheless have these feelings toward colleagues and rivals; if they don't express them directly, they will do it indirectly, often in ways that create still new conflict issues or incur other substantial costs. An example of what is meant by an indirect mode of pursuing a conflict is for Manager A to oppose an expansion plan sponsored by B ostensibly because of inadequate documentation of the proposal, but in reality because B has ignored A on some important occasions in the past.

The immediate emotional energy requirements are a second factor influencing the way conflict is typically managed. It takes emotional energy to totally suppress the conflict and it may take even more emotional energy to confront it. Therefore, conflicts often are played out in some indirect mode, which usually takes the least energy—in the short run. Indirect conflicts, however, have the longest life expectancy, and have the most costs that cannot be charged back against the original conflict. In fact, that is one of the main points of indirect conflict—one does not have to own up to his feelings.

A third factor is consideration of risks associated with organizational conflict. Many important differences over policy and procedure are not surfaced because one or both of the principals fear that the conflict might get out of hand, a residue of interpersonal antagonisms might remain, and they might hurt their careers. These are often realistic fears, but they relate to risks that can be reduced by greater understanding of the ingredients for more effective confrontation and dialogue, and greater skill in supplying these ingredients.

THIRD-PARTY ROLE IN INTERPERSONAL CONFLICT

Third-party roles in the organizational setting have not been institutionalized as they have been in some other social settings, such as labor mediation and conciliation services, the UN Secretariat and its peace-keeping units, marital counseling, and conjoint family therapy. Therefore, third-party functions also are less systematically performed in connection with conflicts in organizations than in these other settings.

Hopefully, one effect of this book will be to accelerate the emergence and development of more systematic third-party roles available as a part of organizational development programs. Also, the insight gained by analyzing the constructive influences of third parties can be used by direct participants to a conflict who want to take steps to break out of the conflict pattern. By understanding the ingredients which third parties may bring to a conflict and the functions they may perform, a participant may in effect simulate a third party, performing the same functions. More than intellectual understanding will be needed, however. The effective use of the knowledge contained in this book requires that human beings develop a capacity to be open and confronting in their encounters with others when the situation calls for it. This is a quality that our child-rearing customs and other social practices have promoted in some, but not most, people. Many organizational development programs in business, government and education, however, are currently operating to develop the interpersonal skills and to create an organizational climate conducive to the methodology of conflict resolution treated here.

Managers of complex organizations show an increasing appreciation for the potential value of persons with a specialized expertise; the scientist in government, the psychologist in business, the economist in labor unions, and the operations researcher in hospitals are all illustrative. Similarly, the systematic use of third-party specialists by any of these types of organizations is increasingly feasible.

The third-party roles and activities examined in this book belong to several families of professional roles. Two deserve mention: first, because of the methodology employed, third-party activities can be regarded as a particular form of "process consultation" which Professor Schein defines as "a set of activities on the part of the consultant which help the client to perceive, understand and act upon process events which occur in the client's interpersonal environment." [2] Second, because of the purpose for which third-party efforts are intended, they constitute a branch of what we shall refer to as "sociotherapy" (i.e., the science or art of treating pathologies or dysfunctions in social relationships). Of particular interest here are such interpersonal patterns as persistent disagreement and

---

[2] Edgar H. Schein, *Process Consultation: Its Role in Organization Development.* Reading, Massachusetts: Addison-Wesley Publishing Company, Inc., 1969, p. 7.

emotional antagonisms that detract from the productivity of the relationship and/or the organization.

THE CONCEPT OF CONFLICT MANAGEMENT

The premise of this volume is *not* that interpersonal conflict in organizations is necessarily bad or destructive, and that third parties must inevitably try to eliminate it or reduce it. In many instances, interpersonal differences, competition, rivalry, and other forms of conflict have a positive value for the participants and contribute to the effectiveness of the social system in which they occur. Thus, a moderate level of interpersonal conflict may have the following constructive consequences: First, it may increase the motivation and energy available to do tasks required by the social system. Second, conflict may increase the innovativeness of individuals and the system because of the greater diversity of the viewpoints and a heightened sense of necessity. Third, each person may develop increased understanding of his own position, because the conflict forces him to articulate his views and to bring forth all supporting arguments. Fourth, each party may achieve greater awareness of his own identity. Fifth, interpersonal conflict may be a means for managing the participants' own internal conflicts.

On the other hand, conflict can be debilitating for the participants, can rigidify the social system in which it occurs, and can lead to gross distortions of reality. Both the nature of the interdependence between the parties and the level of conflict will determine the nature of the consequences for the parties. In the cases analyzed here, there is evidence that the conflict could profitably be better controlled or resolved. We are interested in attempts to facilitate more effective management of the conflict.

One can distinguish between resolution and control as different goals of conflict management. The principals themselves or a third party may attempt to gain *resolution*, so that the original differences or feelings of opposition no longer exist; or they may attempt to merely *control* conflict, so that the negative consequences of the conflict are decreased, even though the opposing preferences and antagonisms persist.

We contemplate a variety of constructive outcomes of interpersonal conflicts, depending upon the basis of the conflict and other circumstances, briefly illustrated as follows: [3]

[3] These do not refer to the cases analyzed in detail in Chapters II–IV of this report.

1. A recurrent conflict between two managers was based on a misunderstanding regarding motives. Confrontation enabled the parties to discover the discrepancy and to establish understanding. In this case, one person had persistently misinterpreted the intentions of the second whom he had seen as trying to get his job.

2. The current and persistent feelings of conflict between two committee members had originated from conflicting interests and pressure conditions which no longer obtained. The cycle of reciprocal distrust and antagonism was finally interrupted by an outside intervention, which facilitated the development of new attitudes more consistent with the current administrative and political realities.

3. Two organization members had personal styles and mutually contradictory role definitions which produced relatively destructive interpersonal conflict. The parties were brought into dialogue to explore their differences in an effort to find some basis for better accommodation. The outcome: although they did not change their respective personal styles of relating, they did modify and integrate their respective role definitions, and eleminated their emotional conflict.

4. Two managers who were in direct competition with each other for a promotion pursued their goals by actions which went beyond competitive striving and involved mutually destructive tactics. With some assistance the parties reached an accord outlawing the destructive conflict tactics.

5. Two bureaucrats were in basic disagreement with each other regarding an important substantive issue of the agency, and the conflict was escalating into personal emotional antagonism. A candid dialogue between them increased their ability to keep separate the substantive conflict and their personal relations.

Each of the above-mentioned conflict episodes involved an interpersonal confrontation which was instrumental in obtaining better conflict control or resolution. By *confrontation* we mean that the parties directly engage each other and focus on the conflict between them. We can suggest the various purposes of such an interpersonal confrontation: to increase authenticity in the relationship and to allow the principals to experience a sense of increased personal integrity; to increase their mutual commitment to improve the relationship; to actually diagnose the conflict; to increase the principals' sense of control over the quality of their relationship; to discover and experiment with ways of de-escalating the conflict.

A PRELIMINARY COMMENT ON THE THREE CASE HISTORIES

The general strategy of this book will be to relate three case histories involving two-party conflict and third-party assistance, which will provide illustrative material and a point of departure for the more abstract and broader analysis of the role of third parties in interpersonal peacemaking.

These three cases are not offered as representative of the full range of interpersonal situations to which our third-party analysis is applicable. While the cases later will be differentiated in many important respects, two conditions common to these three cases deserve preliminary comment.

First, in all three cases the third party was a behavioral science consultant to the organization of which the conflict principals were members. He was an external consultant who was generally identified with an approach to interpersonal relations involving openness and confrontation. Interpersonal openness and confrontation have historically been used in workshops for purposes of human relations training and in that context are a part of a methodology referred to as "sensitivity training" or "T-group Laboratories."

Secondly, the same third-party consultant is involved in all three cases and his general professional identity was perceived in a broadly similar way by all three pairs of conflict principals. The third party in the three cases studied here is a member of an emerging profession of consultants to organizations (and other social systems) whose approach includes, but is not confined to adaptation of the methods, principles, and concepts of sensitivity training. His approach in the present instances also included some adaptation of the methods, principles, and concepts of labor-management mediation, but in general, he was associated in the minds of the principals with the method of sensitivity training. Although the nature of this exposure varied from person to person, a typical experience shared by the principals was a one-week management-development program, usually called a "sensitivity training laboratory." The programs involve low-structured groups (T-groups) in which members help each other learn how each person is perceived by others. In these groups, special attention is usually given to identification of those aspects of an individual's interpersonal style which are self-defeating (e.g., tend to drive others away from himself), and those which are effective (e.g., induce trust). These experiences provided the conflict principals with important practice in being open about one's interpersonal reactions and in engaging in interpersonal confrontation.

While the majority of the conflict principals studied here were not inclined—on their own—to continue to practice openness and confrontation after they returned to their respective organizations, their prior experience made them more responsive to the third party's initiatives involving these elements. We acknowledge that in combination these two conditions—the professional identity of the third party and the prior experiences of the two principals—enhanced the effectiveness of the third party's interventions documented here. This, in itself, has important implications for the practice of organizational development and third-party theory. At the same time, we resist any conclusion that the specifics of these cases constitute necessary preconditions to the effectiveness of the third party's interventions. For example, Chapter 8 analyzes the particular personal and role relationships of the third party which influence his effectiveness in performing each of a variety of third-party functions. That analysis suggests that certain types of organizational superiors, or peers, as well as internal organizational consultants, can play third-party roles in managing interpersonal conflict. The analysis also indicates the types of third-party efforts that can be used to prepare the principals for an interpersonal confrontation when they have not had prior exposure to the general methods which are utilized by the consultant in the confrontation.

THE LEARNING STRATEGY: COUPLING THE ROLES OF PRACTITIONER AND RESEARCHER

I was both *the actor in* the third-party roles in the three cases reported here and *the observer of* the third party's behavior. This duality as practitioner and researcher-theorist has several implications discussed below.

As background to that discussion, it should be noted that during the episodes under consideration, many of the third-party interventions were either reflexive or intuitive. They took on purposive definition only as I subsequently tried to first describe and then explain the interaction behavior, including my own.

Moreover, I did not know I was going to attempt to write up a case until after the confrontation. Of the approximately twelve cases in which I played third-party roles during a period of a year and a half, the particular three cases included in this book were written up in detail for two principal reasons: they happened to occur at times when I found that I could devote the entire week following the confrontation to reconstructing events and analyzing the process; and I intuitively felt that each of these three experiences had a definite instructional value.

The first implication of the dual action-research role was its meaning for me personally. Writing this book on the basis of my own involvement in these interpersonal conflicts provided a great deal of gratification. I derived both the personal satisfaction of making more conceptual and operational sense out of this type of sociotherapy, and the satisfaction of experiencing increased competence in an area of professional activity. Who could ask for anything more?

Second, there are implications for the resulting research output. Behavioral scientists often insist that responsibility for the research and action aspects of a behavioral-science change project be assigned to different persons. Thus, research and action would occur simultaneously in time and place, but would involve two sets of behavioral scientists. The arguments advanced are that this separation allows for more objectivity in the research, and for the integrity and singlemindedness of the action program itself. The approach of the present project was the opposite in the sense that the research and action involved the same behavioral scientist, but the functions were in large part performed at different times and places. Only after a confrontation reported here did the research opportunity occur to me or the researcher role become a salient one for me. Thus, I would argue that the same person often can manage both action and research responsibilities, and with some important advantages as well as disadvantages.

One advantage for this particular research strategy is that by coupling the third-party participant and observer roles, I eliminated the effect of the social-science observer, an effect which is always difficult to discount. Because an observer does not take actions toward others, others have no occasion to act toward him in ways which reveal their feelings about him and what he is doing. Thus, typically, as researcher I had only to understand what was occurring in a system of three persons, all of whom were active and performing functions of immediate consequence in the interaction setting, rather than a system that included a fourth person in a strictly observer role.

I believe that the research strategy of coupling the third-party participant and observer roles, in contrast to separating them, has the following effects on the quality of observations and interpretation:

a) The third-party participant-observer has complete knowledge of the intentions which underlie the actions of the third party.

b) The participant-observer is a better instrument for identifying the specific set of the total numbers of cues in the situation to which the third party is responding, as well as how the third party configured these cues into a diagnosis.

c) The participant-observer is able to recapture alternative behaviors or actions that were considered but discarded by the third party.

d) However, the third-party participant-observer makes less reliable inferences about the many possible effects of the third party's actions. He tends to be more selective in what is observed. Because of his responsibility in the situation, he will have hopes and fears that can result in either over- or underestimation of desired effects; also, he may tend to be less attuned to unexpected results.

e) The participant-observer generally is somewhat less reliable in describing precisely what he did in terms of manifest behavior.

I would conclude that for the type of objectives of the research reported here, the above advantages of coupling the participant and observer roles outweighed the disadvantages. Given that this research effort was intended to develop theoretical ideas and give them operational meaning, rather than to test the relative strength of particular cause-and-effect relationships, it was somewhat more important to have a basis for inferring intention, reconstructing a diagnostic process, and identifying alternatives, than it was to have strict objectivity in recording or inferring effects and an accurate objective description of manifest behavior.

Notwithstanding the above general conclusion, there was a brief but important period in one of the three cases reported here for which, as observer, I was not able to reconstruct the events, including my participant behavior. The period was the emotionally-charged struggle between Mack and Sy at the staff meeting reported in Chapter 3. Every one of my faculties was attuned to the here-and-now process. I behaved intuitively and relied almost exclusively upon my own emotional sixth sense. The support, reassurance, acceptance, and challenge which I felt I had provided each principal, the two of them as a pair, and the total group, were communicated in subtle nonverbal cues or in telegraphic comments that I was not able to isolate for description or analysis later. Thus, it must be acknowledged that, beyond some level of stress in the situation, *if* the stress is shared by the third party, the quality of the documentation of the process will deteriorate when the participant-observer roles are coupled.

Third, in my opinion, the combination of practitioner and researcher improved the former's practices. Both the discipline of developing a relatively complete record of the behavior of the principals and the third party, and the discovery of patterns and meaning in the third party's actions, helped me evolve more sophisticated diagnostic concepts, or at least impressed upon me the critical importance of certain issues. For example, the importance of the symmetry-asymmetry between two conflicting parties increasingly demanded my attention as a theoretical issue (a topic explored in Chapter 6) and, in turn, more of my actions as a third party became attuned to this dimension of the situation. This interaction between behavioral-science theory and practice is encouraging, even if thus far I have only suggested the relationship within one person.

Fourth, as a more general proposition than the one just made, this strategy of practitioner-researcher has the effect of increasing the likelihood that theories are developed with high relevance to the world of action. This heightened probability is an important consideration in view of what I would regard as the modest yield from the fairly massive behavioral-science research over the past two decades.

Fifth, there is a matter of efficiency. It is efficient to allow one person to perform both action and research roles with respect to the same project. It may save both time and money, since it can eliminate confusion as to the respective roles of the participant and the observer, and the risk of interjecting into a three-party situation occasional gratuitous revelations of the observer's reactions.

ON THE GENERALITY OF THE THEORY

Clearly, the general theory and tactics described here are consistent with the practice of at least one sociotherapist, namely that of the author. But circulation of the whole or parts of the manuscript to other professionals who are doing similar work within organizations confirms the author's belief that the theory and practice in general are not idiosyncratic to himself, but also apply to the work of other persons in third-party roles. How many other readers will find that it explicates the third-party functions with which they are familiar.cannot be determined at this point.

While the immediate focus of the present analysis is on interventions into systems of interpersonal conflict, an assumption underlying this book is that many of the basic third-party functions and tactics identified here are applicable in other social conflicts. [4] Therefore, wherever possible, the third-party functions and intervention tactics will be stated abstractly in this book so that it is easier to visualize their potential relevance to two-party conflicts in other settings.

I do have some limited action experience that bears on the question of the generality of the approach described here. I have used the same methodology, the same concepts and techniques in marital peacemaking, and I have used them in labor-management relations (e.g., facilitating a dialogue between a personnel director and local union president where the interpersonal and interinstitutional relationships had both soured over the previous year).

It is important to note that in the latter case of labor-management relations, I have been especially cautious in delimiting the relevance of the theory and techniques spelled out here. My caution will be understood better if we consider the distinctions among three broad mechanisms for settling disputes: power-bargaining, legal-justice and social-science intervention.

If we assume a dispute between two members of an established social unit, the two parties as well as a neutral third party have several contrasting approaches which they may take in settling the dispute. First, invoking a *legal-justice* mechanism, they would ask: What are the rules of this social unit? Applying them to the facts in this dispute, what is the fairest settlement? Second, within a *power-bargaining* approach they would ask: Who is in the most powerful position in this situation? Who could actually force a decision in his favor or at least make it most costly for the other to persist in his position? What settlement is most consistent with the underlying power realities? The third approach, *social-science analysis and intervention*, would take into account many additional facets of the social system and would attempt to find a resolution to the dispute

---

[4] Paralleling this research, some of my other work deals with actual and potential third-party interventions to control or resolve respectively: racial conflict; conflict among Federal agencies in the foreign-affairs community, such as State, AID and Department of Defense; conflict between national factions, in particular the Greek and Turkish Cypriots. Ultimately, I will endeavor to identify similarities and contrasts regarding third-party roles in these widely differing settings.

consistent with the objective of preserving or changing the social system (or certain of its characteristics). [5]

The sociotherapy approach to the third-party role treated here is primarily (but not exclusively) an instance of the third mechanism, social science intervention.

While the three mechanisms are alternatives for use in many conflicts that are handled between two persons, there is a limit to this type of latitude. The nature of the conflict issues, as well as the personal predispositions of the participants, appropriately helps to determine the conflict-resolution mechanism employed. Therefore, in the labor-management setting, I have been especially alert to the possibility that the issues which divided the representatives of these two institutions were either genuine interest conflicts which ultimately would be resolved by power-bargaining, or genuine substantive issues of rights which would ultimately be pursued by legal-justice processes. These other conflict-resolution processes are most appropriate for certain types of conflict for which the methods of sociotherapist—for example, those that promote openness about one's feelings—must be used in a way somewhat more circumscribed than that illustrated in the cases presented in this book.

PLAN OF THE REPORT

Chapters 2 through 4 present the three case histories of interpersonal conflict which provide empirical material for the book. These will be developed generally in a way consistent with the methods used by the third party in gaining understanding of the conflict, its history, and its ramifications. The cases do not follow a common format. Each enables us to illustrate somewhat different aspects of conflict dynamics and third-party functions. Chapter 5 postulates a cyclical model of inter-personal conflict and argues its value as a diagnostic tool. Chapter 6 suggests that well-conceived confrontations can play an important role in the resolution and control of interpersonal conflict and then postulates the strategic functions which third parties can perform. Chapter 7 identifies the tactical interventions of third parties. Finally, Chapter 8 treats the

---

[5] Walton, R. E., "Legal-Justice, Power-Bargaining, and Social-Science Intervention: Mechanisms for Settling Disputes." Institute Paper #194, Institute for Research in the Behavioral, Economic and Management Sciences. Lafayette, Indiana: Purdue University, March, 1968, p. 2.

problem of establishing and maintaining the appropriate third-party role. The general ideas in Chapter 5 through 8 are illustrated by drawing upon and further analyzing the experiences of the third party in the preceding case studies. Chapter 9 summarizes third-party functions, tactics, and desirable role attributes.

2

BILL–LLOYD: NEGOTIATING A
RELATIONSHIP[1]

This chapter reports a conflict between two program directors in a
government agency, and the role played by a third-party consultant. The
confrontation between the principals manifests many of the characteristics
of an interpersonal and intergroup negotiation. The conflict resolution
functions performed by the third party appear to be basic ones deriving
from his role attributes as much as from his active interventions.

BACKGROUND TO THE
CONFRONTATION BETWEEN BILL AND LLOYD

The two principals, Bill and Lloyd, were program directors in the
administrative services component of a large government agency. The third
party to this episode, Dave, was a member of the external consulting staff
of the agency's organizational development program. The organizational
development program emphasized openness of feelings in interpersonal

[1] This chapter is based on an article reprinted by special permission of the Journal of
Applied Behavioral Science; Vol. 4, No. 3, July–August–September, 1968, pp.
327–350.

relations and utilized sensitivity training and team-building experiences. The recently established program had had limited impact on the organization as a whole, but had worked more intensively with the administrative-services component, a fact which influenced the nature and the outcome of this episode.

One of the principals, Bill, was responsible for the development of a new organization system (OSP) to be considered for adoption by the line organization. He had been director of the Information Networks Program for about five months before the confrontation reported here, which occurred in January. (See Fig. 2—1.) During that period he had learned to cope with many frustrating conditions. There was uncertainty whether the system would ever be adopted and when that decision would be made. Moreover, he had to rely on several levels of superiors above him to represent his interests with the high-level official who could make this decision. Communication downward from the top was equally unsettling; there was a continuous stream of reports reaching him and his group, which were interpreted as alternately encouraging and discouraging signs relative to the adoption of the system they were developing. The uncertainty of the program in turn resulted in a high turnover of the better members of his staff. Finally, he had to rely upon another group, the Systems Research Programs Staff (also within the administrative-services component), to supply much of the professional talent required by the project. For several months these factors depressed morale within the professional staff and increased tensions between Bill and George, the section head of the Systems Research Program who was responsible for that group's efforts on OSP.

In October, four months before the episode described here, the combined staffs working on the OSP project, including both Bill and George, had met for two days in an off-site location to "build a team" and accomplish some program task work. Several internal and external consultants on the organizational development staff, including the third-party consultant in this case, participated in the meeting to facilitate the teambuilding process. The meeting helped increase the familiarity, respect, and trust among members of the total group, improve the integration of the two subgroups, and increase staff members' feelings that they were being utilized. Especially important. for Bill was an increased, if not perfect, understanding between himself and George regarding their roles and personal styles. Also, Bill and the total group somehow resolved to prevent the uncertainties of the OSP program from continuing to interfere with their ability to work on the tasks at hand.

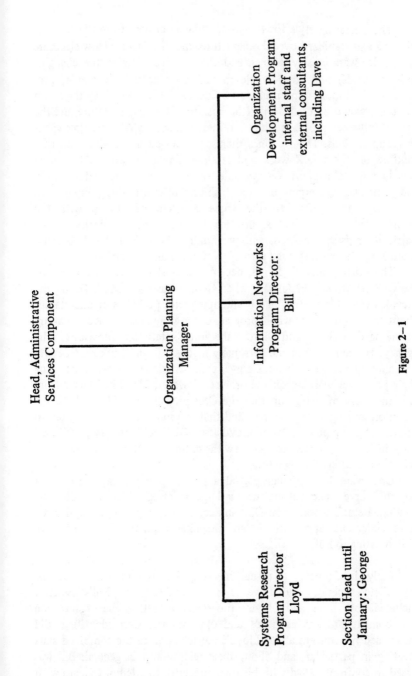

Head, Administrative
Services Component

Organization Planning
Manager

Systems Research
Program Director
Lloyd

Section Head until
January: George

Information Networks
Program Director:
Bill

Organization
Development Program
internal staff and
external consultants,
including Dave

Figure 2–1

The operating style for the group, which emerged from the October meeting and stabilized over the next three months, involved low structure (i.e., roles were loosely defined and changed according to the changing task demands) and considerable mutual influence; for example, professionals had more opportunity to influence the way in which their own resources would be used. In part because the fluid task structure and the mutual-influence process required it, there was somewhat more time spent in group sessions. The meetings themselves moved in the direction of a mixture of direct task work and group-maintenance work. Also, more social-emotional support was available for members who needed it both in the group and in interpersonal relationships. Apparently this group pattern was more appropriate to the triple problem of coping with the environmental stress factors, meeting the needs of a majority of the particular persons involved, and performing the task at hand, because internal operations improved through November and December.

The other principal, Lloyd, became the Systems Research liaison to the OSP effort early in January when George was transferred. During the previous year, Lloyd, too, had been coping with problems of uncertainty about the future of the whole program of his group. He was acutely aware of the need to clarify and improve the group's status and functions in the agency. He had not become personally involved in the work on OSP. He had allowed his subordinate, George, considerable autonomy in handling their personnel working on the project. However, Lloyd had heard from two members of his group that the OSP project still did not have the direction and rigor they desired, and that too much time was devoted to analysis of group process. When Lloyd assumed direct liaison responsibility early in January, he wanted to review the entire OSP project, including the role of his staff and his own role.

One event in particular played a part in precipitating the conflict reported here. The setting was a large meeting which included the combined staffs working on OSP and certain other persons. Lloyd made some statements apparently in an outspoken manner, which were very disconcerting to Bill.

Early in January, a casual meeting occurred involving Bill, his immediate superior, and Dave. The responsibility of Bill's superior included both Bill's and Lloyd's programs, as well as the organization development projects as needs and opportunities were identified. Bill mentioned his concern about Lloyd's participation in the combined staff meeting in particular, and about their relationship in general. Bill was urged to confront Lloyd with his own concerns, to attempt to learn what prompted Lloyd to do what he did in the earlier meeting, and to try to establish a better working relationship. Bill decided to do this, and expressed a desire to have a consultant present. Dave offered to participate.

The following day, Bill first called Lloyd and set up a meeting in his office for later that morning, and then called Dave asking whether he could attend. Dave agreed to attend, asking Bill to be responsible for explaining Dave's presence to Lloyd (who had never met Dave) and for getting Lloyd's concurrence for Dave to be present. Dave further said Bill and Lloyd would have to determine how Dave could be helpful.

The important issue in the case appeared to be that Lloyd was dissatisfied with the role of his staff in OSP, with his role relationship to Bill, and with the operating style of the larger OSP project group, while Bill obviously had been satisfied with these factors. Lloyd's approach was to create an incentive for Bill to review these conditions. The disturbance he caused for Bill in the first combined group meeting he attended had the effect of creating an incentive for Bill to work on their relationship, and perhaps, if necessary, to renegotiate it. Bill acted quickly, partly in order to avail himself of Dave's presence on the scene. In any event, by the time they met in Bill's office, both had decided it was in their respective interests to discuss their relationship, and both were prepared for some form of interpersonal confrontation.

THE CONFRONTATION MEETING

Familiarization

Lloyd and Bill were present in Bill's office when Dave arrived. Bill introduced Dave as a consultant to the organization, whom he had asked to attend, explaining that this was part of a larger pattern of the OSP program which involved using behavioral science consultants whenever possible. He asked if Lloyd approved; Lloyd said he was glad to have Dave present. Dave asked Lloyd if he had attended one of the many sensitivity training workshops which had been sponsored by the organizational development group. Lloyd indicated that he had; and Dave in turn identified himself as a member of the outside consulting organization which had been staffing the agency's sensitivity-training labs. Under the circumstances of this case, this brief interchange tended to go a long way in establishing Dave's identity in a way appropriate for his third-party role. We will analyze this point later.

Bill busied himself on other matters for several minutes, allowing Dave and Lloyd to become acquainted. During this time, Lloyd did almost all of the talking, and Dave the listening. Lloyd discussed education, including his current problem of having a constructive influence on his children's choice in educational institutions. Dave's occasional participation on the topic was directed to the difficulties in the relationship between parents and children in their teens, rather than the relative merits of different educational institutions. As a result of this brief conversation, Dave mentally registered two tentative observations: First, Lloyd can be overpowering in his interpersonal style, with a result that the other person may experience frustration and withdraw or attack. Second, Lloyd may generally tend to resist discussing the more personal aspects of issues, as he did with the question of his children's preference for colleges. Only the first hypothesis tended to be borne out by subsequent developments.

Bill concluded his discussion with his secretary, and the three men moved to sit opposite each other in three comfortable chairs. The first subject of discussion was not topically pertinent to the relationship, and Dave excused himself to leave the room for a few minutes, feeling that the break might help them get down to work when he returned. He also wanted to allow Lloyd a greater opportunity to express to Bill any concerns he might have about his (Dave's) involvement. After Dave returned, they entered upon a discussion of their relationship, and especially Lloyd's role in the OSP program.

The Opening Charges

Lloyd led off with a set of statements which asserted that he was a different person from George, with whom Bill had been dealing, and that he had different views and preferences. Also, in the prelude to his other remarks, Lloyd indicated that he saw some "real gaps in the OSP design" thus far, and was anxious to remedy these if he were involved. His remarks also included the following points:

First, Lloyd charged that his own staff had not been allowed to contribute to the "strategic architectural, broad-design level" of the project; rather, that they had been assigned merely the lower level, "technical-computer work." Then Lloyd said, "Moreover, if this is the type of resource talent you need for the OSP project, perhaps my staff should not be in the business of supplying this type of manpower."

Second, Lloyd observed that the role of his staff had been defined as strictly advisory to Bill's group. Continuing, he said that he did not know whether it was a viable arrangement for his staff to make important contributions of resources without a role in decision making.

Third, he objected to Bill's supervisory pattern, complaining, for example, that the manner in which professionals from the two groups were being assigned tasks allowed him little or no leadership role with respect to his own professionals involved in the project.

Thus, he was charging that his unit's resources were being used below their capacity on the OSP project, that his unit had too little decision influence, and that his leadership position was undermined by the operating style encouraged by Bill. He was indicating that the *status quo* was unacceptable to him. Then he went on to offer an alternative: to "break off" the members of his professional staff utilized by OSP and permanently reassign them to Bill's group. This alternative, Lloyd noted, should be attractive to Bill; it also had the advantage of "freeing up (his program) to do something else, getting new customers."

This latter proposal sounded to Dave more like a bargaining tactic than a seriously proposed solution. It was as if Lloyd had chosen to continue to build pressure on Bill during the confrontation in order to create bargaining leverage and to convince Bill that he could not be taken for granted. Threatening to break off the relationship could be seen as a means of inducing Bill to take a more flexible attitude.

The Counterpoint

After several unsuccessful attempts to break into Lloyd's long presentation of his views, Bill dropped his tactic of trying to respond to Lloyd's points. Instead, he challenged Lloyd directly for not allowing him any opportunity to respond. Lloyd stopped abruptly, acknowledged the appropriateness of Bill's challenge and made a resolution to listen.

Bill then recalled that he "had real trouble" with Lloyd's participation in the large meeting referred to earlier. He said that he had not understood what Lloyd was trying to do. "In fact," he said, "I'm having some of the same reactions to what you have just been saying."

Bill's subsequent statements could be arranged as responses to Lloyd's assertions as follows:

First, Bill said he disagreed with Lloyd's view that computer-technical-mechanical contributions were of a "lower level" than the strategic-architectural-conceptual. Moreover, in his view, Lloyd's staff had been allowed to contribute to the latter.

Second, Bill described his view of the client-consultant roles of the two groups: "Systems Research staff should make resources and advice available to the Information Networks staff who then have final decisions on design and the responsibility for working with the line organization." Thus, he acknowledged the conflict with Lloyd on this point.

Third, Bill defended his working style, claiming that the pattern had not detracted from the leadership role of Lloyd's predecessor, George. Also, he denied that he had given work assignments to personnel in the other group, except as a result of working it out with George. Bill assured Lloyd that he would respond to any concerns of this kind when they arose.

After both persons had had an opportunity to express themselves and make rebuttals Bill turned to Dave and asked him for his observations. Before Dave could respond, Lloyd explained that first he wanted to make another statement. He asked Bill directly whether he would want several members of Lloyd's staff if their positions could be transferred. Bill objected that such a transfer would never be approved and, therefore, he saw no reason to give it further thought. Besides, his need for the talent in question was temporary, which argued against any transfer.

Digging Deeper: From the Intergroup to the Interpersonal Level

When Dave did participate, he suggested that the interchange could be characterized as a negotiation, with Lloyd in effect saying "here are my needs or requests, which must be given due consideration if my staff is going to continue to contribute to OSP." Dave sharpened the three issues which Lloyd had put on the agenda, first citing Lloyd's view and then describing what he heard as Bill's answer, in much the same terms as contained in the report above. After some further discussion of these points, they identified other areas of concern which were probably more basic to the conflict.

Lloyd did not feel comfortable with the operating style of the total OSP group under Bill's leadership: it was too loose, too unstructured, and too "groupy." He preferred more "crispness" and more structure. In contrast, Bill was quite pleased with the group's method of operating, which he thought had been working well and which he found personally satisfying. Bill didn't want Lloyd to try to change the way in which the group operated. He did not react sympathetically to Lloyd's preferences. Therefore, Lloyd indicated with increasing emphasis that he had preferences different from those of his predecessor and that Bill *was* going to have to consider these. In effect, Lloyd wanted the operating methods reconsidered to take into account his own stylistic preferences.

In addition, Lloyd had some general ideas on the OSP, but he had not yet been given enough information about the status of the project in order to test his ideas. Therefore, he wanted to get together soon for a review. Later in the discussion, he acknowledged that one of his underlying concerns was in "getting connected" with the project and also in being recognized as an experienced and competent person on the project team. This need to be seen as competent was underscored in a side conversation with Dave while Bill was handling one of several telephone calls which interrupted the meeting. Lloyd enumerated for Dave many experiences in the past in which he had had full responsibility for developing such systems in other organizations. He noted, in contrast, that members of Bill's group did not have any real practical experience.

Bill, for his part, failed to communicate a direct interest in what Lloyd could contribute, nor did he seem to become fully aware of Lloyd's needs to be recognized in this respect. On the other hand, he felt himself under attack from Lloyd's criticism of the group's efforts to date. It appeared to Dave that Bill's lack of attention to Lloyd's need for recognition might be related to the latter's attacks on the performance of Bill's group, and vice versa. Dave tried to alert the two parties to these more subtle interpersonal issues which could serve to keep them apart.

The outcome of the session was to schedule a meeting of both groups to review the work and to further explore how they could and should work together on OSP. As the session concluded, Bill expressed satisfaction with the meeting, indicating that he felt there was more understanding. Dave asked to meet with each person to discuss the meeting and to determine whether he could be of any further help. Both agreed that this was desirable.

The two principals had styles and skills that increased the likelihood of a successful confrontation. Although Lloyd often appeared dominating in interpersonal discussion, and although he sometimes resisted more personal interpretations of his own behavior, he had a directness and strength that was consistent with direct interpersonal confrontation. For Bill's part, his general skill at understanding the interpersonal process made him better able not only to hear Lloyd out, but also to challenge the latter's occasional domineering manner.

The third party performed a diagnostic function during and after the confrontation. He listened to each of the disputants discuss his views and feelings, and sharpened what he understood to be an issue, to which the participants responded in ways which tended to confirm or disprove that this was the underlying issue. An effort was made to state these issues in ways which made each person's position understandable, legitimate, and acceptable. One apparent effect of this understanding, legitimating, and sharpening of issues, was to encourage Lloyd then to identify the more personal concerns he had about not being involved and not being recognized as a competent person with experience relevant to OSP.

The third party chose to play what he regarded as a minor role in regulating the process. Essentially, he let the parties run on their own. For example, he waited for Bill to deal first with the way Lloyd was dominating the discussion. Thus, he believed that the two parties had an opportunity to reveal or develop their own interaction equilibrium. Nevertheless, Lloyd attributed an active role to Dave. After reading this report he said,

> I believe the report understates Dave's effect as a third party and casts him more outside the process than I experienced him. Both his presence and his active, constructive participation influenced the process. For example, he turned me off once when I was getting long-winded, reminding me of the need to listen. When you hear something from a third party who doesn't have an investment in the issues at stake, you are more likely to respond to that advice, especially if it is given to you in a timely way on the spot. . . . In sum, for me, he was not only a catalytic agent, but also an ingredient in the situation.

POST-CONFRONTATION REACTIONS AND DEVELOPMENTS

Late that afternoon, Bill told Dave in convincing terms that the session with Lloyd had been productive. He believed that as a result of the confrontation he and Lloyd understood each other better and could maintain a dialogue on the outstanding issues between them. In his opinion, the presence of the consultant had made a great difference in encouraging a genuine confrontation; for example, he stated that if Dave had not been there, he probably would not have challenged Lloyd "at the process level" on the way the latter was dominating the discussion.

Several days later, Dave telephoned Lloyd to learn his reactions to the confrontation meeting, to inquire about subsequent developments, and to offer his further assistance if it should be desired. The review meeting between the two groups had occured in the meantime. From Lloyd's report it was clear that some of the differences between Bill and himself remained, but also that the two men had a better basis for managing these differences.

Lloyd's remarks indicated continued but reduced concerns about whether the resources of his staff were being used productively, and whether his group was "too far in or too far out" of OSP. He showed increased understanding of the operating style of the combined groups by commenting on how this had been influenced by the great uncertainty under which this development work was being conducted. He continued to be critical of some aspects of the OSP as it stood currently and of the "cold hard fact that Bill doesn't have anyone on his staff that has been through this." He added, however, that he didn't think his own group "could make it *in toto*, either."

He, also, now had reason not to press for an immediate resolution of certain intergroup issues involving the respective roles of the two groups. Apparently, in talking with his superior, he gained a better appreciation of the provisional nature of the composition and leadership of the development effort. He seemed satisfied that if and when there was a decision to go ahead on the project, a definite structure would be created, and that the present structure would not prejudice the form that the eventual one would take.

Lloyd commented about the effect of the confrontation on his relationship with Bill:

I think we have made headway . . . I feel more relaxed about the way things are going . . . I came away from the meeting with a better understanding of Bill's position (as a matter of fact, I stressed him a little bit to get him to be explicit) . . . and I know Bill better understands my position. I know this because at the larger group meeting Bill made a summation of the discussion we had in his office and I was satisfied with it; he was able to accurately state my position . . . we have openness going for us . . .

Lloyd believed that Dave had been helpful and that it would be desirable to keep a consultant involved "who was familiar with the developing situation, but who could take a spectator position."

Several months later, Bill read this report and added,

Against a longer time frame, the results were even better than the report conveys. As a human being, Lloyd is accustomed to more structure than we had in the total group. Nevertheless, within a month, we were operating very well, and he felt as much at home as anyone. Through understanding the personal needs he communicated during that session in January, we found that his participation in the project became both visible and valued.

Dave also learned that Lloyd had developed high regard for Bill over the same period.

CONCLUSION

What were the potential and actual outcomes of the Bill—Lloyd confrontation? Against the background of possible mounting tension, it reversed the cycle and achieved a trend of de-escalation. The immediate effect was to help the parties clarify the intergroup issues. For example, Lloyd cited Bill's ability to state his (Lloyd's) position as evidence that Bill understood. They made even more rapid progress in eliminating the interpersonal conflict: within a couple of weeks Lloyd reported feeling more relaxed, and noted that he and Bill "have openness going for us." Later Bill reported that within a month Lloyd "felt as much at home as anyone" with Bill's operating style and that Lloyd's participation had become "both visible and valued." The improved rapport between the directors enabled them to handle more effectively whatever intergroup issues remained.

This was a successful interpersonal confrontation in which the third party had a constructive influence on the outcome. The third party's influence resulted in part from his more active contributions (some regulating of the interaction, sharpening issues, and diagnosing the relationship). More surprising were the basic functions he performed in a passive way—by his mere presence. His function in encouraging the confrontation in the first place derived from the participants' expectations about him (support, process skill, learning, and insight) and from the symbolic meaning attributed to him as a result of his identification with a class of persons (sensitivity trainers) with whom the participants had had an intensive and successful experience. In the following two cases, active interventions into the ongoing process and individual work with the participants were more important aspects of the third-party role than in this case.

3

MACK–SY: CONFRONTING
A DEEPLY FELT CONFLICT

The conflict reported here occurred between the controller and assistant director of an equipment manufacturing division of a large firm. As in the preceding case, the conflict has both interpersonal and interdepartmental aspects. However, the interpersonal and, in particular, the emotional dimensions are relatively more salient in the conflict analyzed in this chapter. The third-party consultant played an active role in the phases of the conflict episode which took place during two visits to the organization over a period of four months.

The chapter provides a background description of the organization and an account of the conflict. The latter covers first the consultant's interviews with each party prior to their interpersonal confrontation; second, their dialogue at cocktails after work on Wednesday; third, the emotional conflict in the staff meeting on Thursday morning; fourth, the impromptu period of rest and recuperation at the club Thursday afternoon; fifth, the consultant's final contacts with the principals before departure; sixth, further developments, including a reconciliation of the parties.

BACKGROUND TO THE CONFRONTATION
BETWEEN SY AND MACK

Organizational Setting

The immediate organizational context for the conflict between Sy (the assistant director) and Mack (the controller) was the management staff for the Indianapolis operations of the corporation. Corporation headquarters, as well as marketing and research functions, were located in Detroit. A particular line of consumers' products was processed and manufactured at Indianapolis. In addition, a smaller volume of industrial products was both produced and sold by the Indianapolis organization. The general manager's staff consisted of the persons shown on the organization chart in Fig. 3–1, with the exception of the industrial equipment sales manager.

The turnover of executives in these positions was quite rapid. None of the members of the present staff had been in his present position more than one year. Most of the persons they had replaced were promoted to positions in other operations, or to higher management positions in Detroit. Two who had not been promoted had left the company. All members of the present staff were aspiring to higher positions. However, in no case were they assured of a future promotion; each of the managers was assumed to have strengths and weaknesses. All were aware of the "up or out" character of Indianapolis assignments.

Promotions in this situation were heavily influenced by two factors: First, it was crucial for one to have a sponsor two or more levels above him; a typical pattern was for a manager who had been promoted to continue to look out for the welfare of a former subordinate whom he liked and regarded highly. Second, the director at a division like Indianapolis was a key person. Because of the geographic separation between Indianapolis and Detroit, the director was the primary source of information about, and evaluation of current performance of, members of his staff. Thus, to be promoted, a manager at Indianapolis usually had to have *both* a sponsor in Detroit and the positive evaluation of the director.

Dave's contact with the division had begun fifteen months earlier at the initiative of the previous division director. During his consulting visits, he observed staff meetings and led critiques of the group process. The primary purpose of such a review was to improve the functioning of the group. Dave also met with staff members individually, discussing their respective organizational or interpersonal problems or concerns, and sharing his own reactions and perceptions of them based on the staff meeting they had both attended.

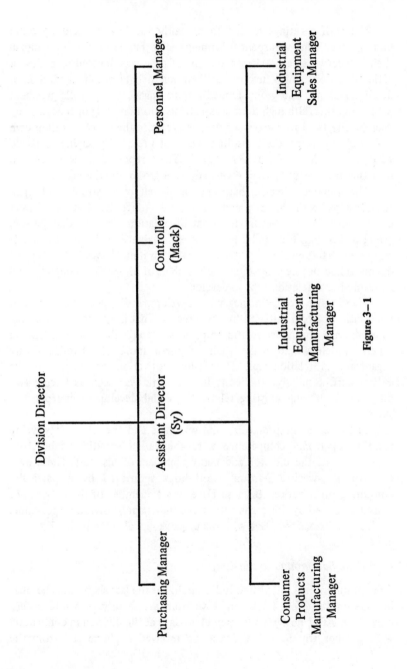

Figure 3–1

The staff meetings tended to be fairly low-key, marked by some humor. Much time was spent informing each other about developments in their respective areas. A lesser amount of time was devoted to policy or action questions which involved deliberation, debate, recommendation, or decision-making. The group tended *not* to engage in open disagreement with each other, although there was a stated norm favoring openness. They occasionally tried to review, analyze, and react to the process of their own staff meeting when the consultant was not present by saying "let's do what we would if Dave were here." They reported some success in initiating and executing their own analysis of group functioning.

The present director had developed relatively strong and open relationships with most members of his staff. He initiated direct discussions with a subordinate about his relationship with that person, giving and asking for candid reactions and evaluations. Many of his staff expressed high respect and personal warmth for him. However, this type of openness had not developed among members of his staff, although he said he wanted such relationships to develop.

There was a strong "management development" aspect to this type of relationship pattern initiated by the director. That is, in addition to trying to establish a productive relationship, he wanted feedback for himself and others, which would make each of them more effective in future organizational relationships. This latter motivation was shared by the entire staff. Similarly, the consultant's work was seen as having two purposes—improving existing relationships and developing interpersonal skills.

Instrumental in promoting the openness and the desire to develop more interpersonal competence were the earlier sensitivity laboratory experiences of the director and many members of his staff. These were one- or two-week "T-group" workshops sponsored by a particular consulting organization. Because Dave was a member of the network of consultants used by this organization, the Indianapolis division's personnel in this case associated Dave with the processes involved in their laboratory experiences.

Immediate Background to the Conflict

The consultant had not visited Indianapolis for the last six months because he was on the West Coast on leave from the faculty of a midwestern university. After he agreed to spend two days at the division in connection with another trip to the Midwest, he received a phone call from the director, who discussed some of the problems among the staff. The director emphasized that the current organizational environment included many uncertainties. The performance of the division was below expectations, due in part to operations at Indianapolis and in part to other factors not within the direct control of the division staff. In addition, a power struggle had developed within the higher management staff in Detroit to which the director reported organizationally. Despite the fact that the director had received favorable and approving signals from his direct superior and his superior's boss, he was feeling some personal stress and insecurity created by the general situation.

Still other uncertainties were generated by recent changes he had made within the division, involving the reporting relationship of two persons on his staff: the sales and production managers of industrial equipment both had reported directly to him and now reported to the assistant director. (See Fig. 3-1.) One was removed from the director's staff, namely the industrial equipment sales manager. Both felt that they had suffered "setbacks." The changes had created strains in the director's relationships with the two persons involved. The man removed from the staff had been strongly dressed down by the director for his performance.

The director commented on each member of his staff. He commented on Sy (the assistant director) indicating high satisfaction with his development, and noted that Sy was serving as his primary sounding-board and colleague. He also commented on Mack (the controller), whom he assumed for the moment Dave hadn't met, because Mack had been promoted to the staff position just prior to Dave's last visit to Indianapolis. His comments were:

Mack is a young fellow who doesn't want to be controller. He is aggressive and competent. He is so damned aggressive that he often drives people out of a discussion. That even happens to me. I'll leave a discussion with him all frustrated. But he just got back from a sensitivity training lab and he said he got feedback from his T-group about his aggressiveness. We just had a wonderful lunch together and he reported his lab experience. He also reported that during a very difficult episode in the T-group he had waited and then come quietly into the discussion and to his surprise they had listened to him and took his ideas. I .was pleased that he had that lesson. However, in a recent meeting, he reverted back to type, and became aggressive.

The director also reported an episode in the last staff meeting.

Yesterday Sy and Mack were having a conflict. Sy brought it into the open. He had put on the agenda "controller responsibility." This was the first I knew about it—when I saw it on the agenda. Mack contended his job was to give figures upward, not downward. Sy couldn't buy this. One of Sy's subordinates had raised the issue in the first place and had gotten together with Sy to put it on the agenda. In the meeting, this subordinate said that the controller area was a service area and that his employees shouldn't have to wait. They weren't getting service. Well, I broke in and tried to set this fellow straight; I said, "When you vie for service, you still have to get it through persuasion." This may have been a little hard on him, but a few days earlier I had said to him, "Can you take it? Do you want me to let you know what I think?" And he had said, "Yes."

The above comment was the director's only reference to the Sy—Mack conflict. In mentioning it and presumably in living it, he had allowed the matter quickly to give way to an interchange between himself and another person.

On the first day of the consultant's two-day visit, he maintained a schedule of discussions with as many members of the staff as possible. During his interviews with Mack and Sy, Dave only vaguely recalled the director's fleeting description of their conflict at the last staff meeting. He had no particular plans to work on this interpersonal relationship.

INTERVIEW WITH MACK

Much of the session with Mack centered in his recent lab experience. The episodes he related had personal significance for him, and Dave found it easy to listen empathically. Mack's references to his present work situation centered on his attitude toward his current job, and his concern with his work relationships. The following concerns and ideas were expressed, but not pursued, in the time available.

Mack felt there was a very bad fit between his personal style and his current job as controller: he tended to be "intuitive," whereas the job required more compulsive behavior. Prior to becoming controller, he had been in the production organization. He questioned that he should ever have been given the controller assignment even though it was a promotion. Apparently, he now felt that he had been pressured into taking the assignment. Also, he was very disappointed that a project (X-Mill project) for which he had been responsible was taken away. After he had pursued it as an acquisition problem, the project was given to Sy as a start-up and operational problem. Mack had wanted to continue with it and believed he was competent to do so.

He indirectly implied that he had withdrawn some energy from his work, reporting, for example, that he put in less time outside regular office hours than formerly. He attributed this change in his life pattern, which his wife applauded, to insight and perspective gained from the T-group, but the context of his remark suggested it was at least partly a result of his disappointment about losing the X-Mill project.

On a positive note, the T-group experience had increased Mack's interest in working on the organizational and personal development of his own subordinates. This newly developed interest served as an outlet for his commitment and imagination—resources which would have been invested in the X-Mill project.

Mack was perplexed about how much of the openness and spontaneity he had learned in the T-group could be used in the organizational situation. He reported that in two instances subsequent to the T-group, his open, expressive behavior toward colleagues had made them quite uncomfortable. Also, he felt an "intense conflict" with another person in the staff group, whom he "knew" he "had to confront"; to date, he had not been ready to follow through. He asked Dave for his advice on how to apply the T-group learning. Dave suggested that there was an optimum time lag after a lab before undertaking work on tough interpersonal issues:

> On the one hand, you need to be back in the organization long enough so that you can differentiate between the behavior norms and the personal risks associated with the temporary T-group and the realities of this permanent organization. On the other hand, you need to act before the excitement of the T-group experience wears off and while you are still more ready to take personal risks.

Because of time limitations and because Mack did not offer to identify the person with whom he was in conflict, the matter was dropped. Later, it became apparent that he was referring to his relationship with Sy.

INTERVIEW WITH SY

Sy had also attended a sensitivity lab since Dave had last talked with him, but it was not especially salient for Sy because it had been four months earlier. Sy identified several areas where he wanted to improve his interpersonal effectiveness; he was not satisfied with his relationships with subordinates; he had not yet established a relationship with the new personnel manager; finally, he was "especially concerned" about his poor relationship with Mack. The remainder of the session dealt with Sy's conflict with Mack.

Sy mentioned that he and Mack were very different, and Dave asked Sy to elaborate. That particular effort quickly gave way, as Sy began describing Mack and his own reactions to him.

In Sy's opinion, Mack was not sufficiently interested in the success of the division's operations and was too concerned directly about his own career. Although it was not clear what events or patterns Sy had in mind, it later occurred to Dave that Sy could have been referring to several different things. First, the director (but not Sy) had mentioned a recent incident in which Mack had complied with the preferences of the corporate controller in Detroit who wanted him to delay making operating performance data available to the division staff and the director's line superior. Second, Sy himself later clarified how much he resented the fact that, while the operations in general and he in particular needed more controller work, Mack was worrying less about doing his immediate job than whether he should be in that job. Third, Sy was also personally inconvenienced and annoyed by the fact that when he assumed responsibility for the X-Mill project, Mack essentially "washed his hands" of the matter, withholding any assistance.

Sy said that he resented Mack's attempt to dominate a discussion "even when Mack is knowledgeable on the subject." Sy cited a recent discussion in which he was trying to get as much assistance as possible from Mack. Paradoxically he, Sy, ended the discussion because of Mack's manner, even though he knew he was dependent upon Mack for information and advice.

After Sy seemed to have exhausted his perceptions of and concerns about Mack, Dave said,

> You know, I'm sitting here considering the difference in our reactions to Mack. Earlier today I had a session with Mack in which I reacted very positively and felt quite friendly toward him. It's true it was just one session, and a special type at that, but I wonder what unique aspects of your relationship with Mack account for your feelings toward him.

Shortly afterwards, Dave added, "I wonder what *you* bring to that relationship." He also shared with Sy another question he was pondering, "Given your long list of different negative feelings about Mack, is one of these basic and the others just reflections of this central concern? Do you have any good hunches on this question?"

Sy joined in the discussion of this question with an exploratory attitude. His own hypothesis seemed to center on the "trust" issue. He related an instance where he deliberately had not consulted Mack in making a decision to promote a man who had recently been Mack's subordinate. Sy acknowledged that it would have been natural and appropriate for him to consult Mack on this matter. However, he did not even inform him that he was considering the promotion, "I guess because I didn't trust him to keep it to himself." Sy concluded that he was going to have to confront Mack and have it out with him.

It was at this point that Dave began to actively consider the idea of working with the two men as a pair during his visit. The original timetable had scheduled all of Dave's time. However, it was 4:45 p.m. and perhaps plans could be changed to accommodate a get-together over drinks after work. Without yet deciding to try to arrange for a confrontation, he shared the idea with Sy. Sy responded favorably, even though he would have to shift some important family commitments. Dave himself felt ambivalent. He walked over to look in Mack's office and confirmed that Mack was still there. Dave asked himself, "Is Mack ready? Are Sy and Mack going to confront anyway? Do I want to be responsible? How much energy do I have available after a strenuous day and several days before that?"

Arranging for the Principals to Meet

Dave decided to meet if Mack was available. He communicated this decision to Sy, who immediately went to Mack's office to invite him to meet for drinks. Although at that point Dave did not perceive that he had any choice in the matter, he wondered whether it would have been better for him (rather than Sy) to have invited Mack. Sy returned to indicate that they had agreed to meet at 5:30 p.m. at the club.

Dave informed Sy that the personnel manager, who expected to meet Dave after work, would probably join them at the club. Dave informed the personnel manager of the change in plans and explained briefly that he hoped Sy and Mack could work on what appeared to Dave to be important interpersonal issues. The personnel manager offered to stay away, but Dave said he wanted him there because he thought he might be helpful, and because it would assist the personnel manager in building an internal consulting role.

MEETING AFTER WORK: TRYING TO GET THE ISSUES JOINED

After all four persons had arrived and engaged in some chitchat, Dave said, "My thinking about this meeting included the possibility that we do some work on relationships."

After a pause, Sy turned to Mack, "I feel antagonistic toward you, and find it very difficult to work with you. I want to understand why and do something about it if possible."

Mack reacted quickly. His response took the form of emphasizing that he and Sy are very different in their respective styles of working: he is intuitive, Sy is methodical; he tries to make money for the company by spending money, Sy by saving money; he implied that he had a broad view, while Sy was a detail man. His discussion then turned to center on himself: the bad fit between his style and his controller's job; and his recent disappointment in losing the X-Mill project; etc.

Mack went on at some length. Although it is not fully apparent from the above summary of Mack's response, at the time it appeared to Sy, Dave, and the personnel manager that Mack was no longer responding directly to Sy. The personnel manager finally interrupted Mack.

The personnel manager: You are not responding to Sy and his feelings. (There was a scolding tone to the statement.)

Mack: What do you mean?

Dave: You seemed to be describing a constellation of factors impinging upon yourself. Can you link that up to your relationship with Sy?

Mack's response indicated reluctance to confront Sy, and he suggested it was up to Sy to proceed if he liked. Sy then repeated a theme which had occurred in his earlier discussion with Dave.

Sy: I don't know why you bug me; it is more than that we are different .... Is it that I don't like you trying to dominate me, or could it be that I don't trust you? (Mack did not respond.)

Dave (to Sy, who seemed to be disappointed that Mack hadn't responded): Actually there is not much Mack can do with the question phrased that way. Can you supply more of the perceptions and other background upon which your feelings are based?

In reply to Dave's request for him to cite instances that had influenced his attitude toward Mack, Sy recalled that he had not consulted Mack regarding the promotion of a former subordinate of Mack's, "apparently because of a lack of trust." Mack, in turn, confirmed that he did indeed resent not being informed and that he had not understood why Sy hadn't contacted him.

Later, Sy identified another type of issue. Sy stated, "We need more controller work, more data for us in production, more reporting relevant to expenses." Mack's response was along the lines of, "You, Sy, do more controller's work than I do. You go over reports so thoroughly that I count on you to catch errors. Also, it's up to you to decide what your problems are. I've done all a controller can do."

Both this interchange and the preceding one seemed only to scratch the surface of the issues or feelings involved. Sy tried still another issue.

Sy: One thing I can't accept is your response to the X-Mill project. I *need* you to help me with that project. You've got the background information and the abilities which are needed. But when you didn't get overall responsibility for the project, you withdrew completely. I just can't accept your saying, "If I'm not *the* man, I won't contribute."

Mack: But that's how I am. That's how I feel. (Sy's shoulders slumped and he turned the palms of his hands upward in a gesture of futility.)

Dave (both to give Sy some support and to confront Mack): It's hard to deal with that position.

At a later point, as if to suggest that one of the reasons he could not contribute to the X-Mill project had to do with his feelings toward Sy in particular, Mack said, "I must say that I'm concerned about working *for* you when that happens." (Mack was referring to the highly likely development that Sy would be promoted to division director when the present director was promoted or transferred, probably within a year or so.)

Mack was paged for a telephone call, and while he was out of the room, the other three sat silent for a moment. Dave asked Sy, "How do you feel? Do you feel that you and Mack have engaged each other this evening, or have been semi-engaged, or not at all?" Sy responded, "Semi-engaged."

When Mack returned, Dave reported his question to Sy and Sy's answer, and then asked Mack how he felt. He, too, felt "semi-engaged" with Sy.

Both said that this had represented the start of a necessary dialogue and wanted to keep working on the issue when there was an opportunity. Dave later realized that it might well have been advisable to encourage them to agree upon a specific time to meet and resume their dialogue.

The meeting was ended because Sy, Dave, and the personnel manager all had to leave for other engagements. During the phone call, Mack had had his evening appointment cancelled so that he was free the rest of the evening. Dave explained why he had to leave, and also that Sy had indicated to him earlier that he had to leave. (Dave was concerned that Mack did not feel rejected.)

Dave was driven to his motel by Mack, who said that he felt the confrontation was cut short. He had much stronger feelings about Sy which had not come out yet, and he had very deep concerns about what would happen if Sy became the director and, thus, his boss. On the other hand, in response to a direct question from Dave, he said that he did not feel that he was taking great personal risks in the confrontation. Dave was somwhat confused by Mack's last response, but there was no time to pursue it then.

STAFF MEETING: THE CONFRONTATION

Precipitating events

Thursday morning was the regularly scheduled weekly staff meeting. The director and six members of his staff were present: only one member (the consumer products manager) was absent. It was a typical meeting up to the point late in the meeting when a confrontation occurred between Sy and Mack. Several agenda items were discussed in a very businesslike manner. However, certain events or processes appeared to be related to the Sy–Mack relationship. First, Mack shared with the staff the contents of a controller's "confidential" report, noting that his disclosures were contrary to the preferences of higher controller officials in Detroit. The act was significant because of past charges that he was too oriented to higher officials in Detroit, and not concerned enough with the interests of his immediate associates in Indianapolis. Dave interpreted (to himself) the act as a conciliatory overture to Sy and the group.

The second event was an instance where Mack was quite aggressive. The topic being discussed was the need for a general manager for the industrial products operations, which were showing up poorly in the performance record. As pointed out above, the sales and manufacturing managers of industrial products had both reported to the director until recently when an organizational change resulted in their reporting to Sy, as the assistant director. There had been a general assumption that a separate general-manager position ought to be created. The major constraint was that neither the present sales manager nor the manufacturing manager was deemed qualified to handle the general-manager job. Mack pressed the director, challenged his assumptions, and told him what he ought to do, in fact, what he should have been doing. The director showed constraint and was able to use Mack's ideas without fighting Mack or rejecting useful ideas out of defensiveness. However, Mack's aggressiveness in this interchange with the director may have triggered something within Sy which later contributed to his outburst at Mack.

At the conclusion of the business meeting, Dave led a critique of the group's processes. Dave compared the meeting with earlier staff meetings he had observed when the group had a somewhat different composition. The meeting had been relatively uneventful, and Dave's observations sharpened only a few procedural issues or interpersonal interchanges, including the one mentioned above between Mack and the division director. Mack again made a powerful, repetitive, insistent, but somewhat general, assertion to the director that the need was great because the industrial operations were doing so badly.

SY'S OUTBURST AND THE INTERCHANGES
WHICH FOLLOWED

Mack was still going strong when Sy interrupted him with an almost violent outburst, pounding the table, turning toward Mack and slamming his fist down on the table in front of Mack. Sy was obviously very, very angry at Mack.

Sy: Damn it, you keep saying that (that the industrial operations are going badly), but when I try to get you to work on it you don't!

Mack: Wait a minute, the last time I tried in the meeting a week ago—it was *you* that didn't want to continue!

Sy (countering): I broke off the meeting when I couldn't absorb any more.

Sy and Mack argued further on the same point for a brief period. Then Mack shifted the focus and repeated twice his personal feelings about the controller's work and his suitability for that job. Then, Dave confronted Mack with the fact that he had again turned attention to his job when his relationship with Sy was being discussed.

Dave: I have come to a new hunch about your behavior. Are you trying to *prove* that you are *not* suited for the controller's job? . . .There are two hypotheses. First, that you are trying to minimize the effects of the mismatch between your style and the controller job. Second, that you are trying to illustrate, dramatize, demonstrate and prove the mismatch.

Mack: I am trying to minimize the effects of the mismatch, but it's true that I have started to evaluate whether this company is the place for me. (He went on to say that it might be wise for him to consider another firm.)

Sy: I believe it's the second of Dave's hypotheses: that you are trying to convince others of the mismatch. (Sy elaborated on this perception.)

Dave (to Mack): It's possible that at some level you really are trying to make this point, whatever the consequences.

Then at another point, Dave attempted to assess the mutuality of their feelings of dependence on each other:

Dave (to Mack): Do you feel dependent on Sy? He has said he feels dependent on you, but I haven't heard you say anything like that.

Mack: No, I don't.

Dave: To the extent that you have defined the situation in that way, it's very difficult to work on this thing.

The staff meeting interchanges recorded above are only those excerpts from the meeting which Dave could later recall with any degree of clarity. They fail to communicate the extent to which this was a sustained, highly-charged important confrontation of two human beings for each of whom the other was not only an objectively important associate, but must have also represented some psychologically important set of characteristics. Dave's attention was thoroughly occupied by what was happening among Sy and Mack and himself; however, at one point when he quickly checked the others at the round table, he observed that their faces reflected deep concern, involvement, and struggle. None of them ventured into the conflict during this session.

At the end of the staff meeting Dave made the following remarks to the pair and to the others present.

I'm not sure there is a solution. Mack, the fact that you don't feel dependent on Sy makes it more difficult. You are both strong and you are both open about your negative feelings–these are the encouraging factors. One of the problems is that your personal styles may clash so much that you generate new interpersonal issues, even while you're talking and trying to work out existing differences. That's where others can help.

Sy and Mack have different things to offer this staff. It would be a shame for the organization to lose Mack. Mack has certain unique strengths to offer. It's a challenge to find a way to make it possible for Mack to work on Sy's task problems. In part, it's up to you, Mack, to say how others can help make it possible for you to work productively. It is important for the two of you to keep talking. . . .

In concluding the staff meeting, Dave suggested that they all go to lunch; the director suggested they go to the club. On the way out of the office building, the personnel manager said to Dave, "I was moved; that's all I can say." All six rode to the club together.

Before the staff meeting, no one but Sy was aware of the full depth of his negative feelings toward Mack. The director had only mentioned the earlier debate between Sy and Mack. The personnel manager had not made any mention of this conflict in sharing with Dave his perceptions of the current personal and organizational issues. Nor had Dave fully appreciated the depth of Sy's feeling until the staff meeting outburst. Prior to that, when Sy had said to Dave, "I wonder why I feel the way I do toward Mack," he appeared to be puzzled or perplexed, but not highly disturbed.

Sy's tension level had mounted after the evening meeting, apparently out of frustration in failing to engage Mack. This frustration, plus Mack's further provocative behavior during the staff meeting, must have led to Sy's outburst, which in turn pushed the overall tension level to a very high point. This intense confrontation was a climax of the mutual antagonism, and undoubtedly set the background not only for the quiet reflective work that afternoon, but also for the improvements which were to come much later.

REST AND RECUPERATION AND REPAIR OF
THIRD PARTY'S RELATIONSHIP TO MACK

After they had arrived, ordered drinks and handled some miscellaneous business items, the director asked Dave what the group should talk about.

Dave deliberately tried to avoid further work on the Sy–Mack relationship during that luncheon period. Therefore, he raised a question about the pattern of his future work with the staff, suggesting two or three alternative patterns. As a part of the discussion which followed, they explored a misunderstanding. Apparently, the personnel manager had misinterpreted the staff's interest in getting Dave to come several weeks earlier. One person questioned the personnel manager, asking whether he was on board with the idea of having Dave work with the staff. The personnel manager said he definitely was in agreement. Dave himself expressed some irritation with the way the personnel manager had handled the visit, and chided him for being a "hard-nosed negotiator." (In this interpersonal interchange, Dave was a principal. That fact may have facilitated what followed.)

Mack commented that he believed last night had been "rigged." At first, Dave was taken aback by the comment. Addressing himself to Mack, Dave reconstructed his own thinking and his discussions with Sy and the personnel manager which had led to the evening meeting. Dave confirmed that the dialogue had been planned for, but did not accept that it had been "rigged." Nevertheless, Mack added, "I'll never trust you again."

As the group moved from the cocktail lounge to the luncheon table, Dave commented in a half-humorous way to the group, including Mack, "I thought it was clear that I had a white hat. Now I learn that Mack saw me as wearing a black hat."

Mack then reflected ambivalence about the episode by saying, "This type of candid reaction to me and my style of operating is precisely what I wanted from my sensitivity-training group, but didn't get."

There were long lapses of conversation during the cocktail session and the protracted lunch that lasted to mid-afternoon. People were reflecting upon the morning confrontation and its meaning for them, and generally resting by engaging in light conversation. The additional discussion directly relevant to the Sy–Mack episode dealt with Mack's ambivalence about the confrontation and his feelings about Dave's role in it.

Dave (to Mack): I'm concerned about the trust issue. That hits me in the most crucial aspect of my role with this group. I'd like to hear more about what you're thinking or feeling.

Mack: It's not really trust. I just don't know. I've taken some big risks. My own career's on the line. At least my future with this company.

Dave: What is the risk? How is it likely to affect your future with the company?

Mack: Sy will remember this. He can't help but take it into account. It's bound to work against me.

Dave: I see what you mean . . . . Only the future will tell. There just is no way for us to know now. Asking Sy still wouldn't give you an answer to this . . . . but for what it's worth, my sense of Sy's integrity, his discipline, his notions of fairness, these all tell me that he won't use this interchange or what you revealed about yourself against you . . . . In fact, as I reflect on it, maybe you are projecting some of your own inclinations onto Sy. In a way, compared with you, Sy is less likely to be worrying about his career and thinking politically.

Dave (to Mack after some time lapse): As for how you perceive my role in this confrontation, let me add still more detail about what preceded the decision to try and get some dialogue going between you and Sy. When I was talking with Sy yesterday afternoon and he was describing his negative reactions to you, I admitted to him that I didn't have the same reaction to you. I had felt quite positive to you on the basis of our interview; therefore, I said to Sy, I wonder how much of that is Mack and how much is you, Sy.

Notwithstanding his anxiety about the risks he had taken in the confrontation, Mack signalled in several ways that he wanted Dave to continue to work with the staff, with himself, and perhaps also with his subordinates.

Dave's suggestion that they go to lunch together held the group intact following their high emotional experience; this allowed members to provide each other with the reassurance they needed. Also, each member of the group was given an opportunity to individually reflect on the experience and find some meaning for himself. Fortunately, the director and other members of the staff manifested a mature acceptance of the morning's confrontation. This undoubtedly went far in reducing the fears of disapproval which the participants might otherwise have entertained.

TOUCHING BASES BEFORE DEPARTURE

When the group returned to the office, Dave dropped in on each of them before he departed.

In Sy's office, Sy said, "I need to improve my ability to confront and talk through an issue."

Dave was reassuring. "You have come a long way. The important thing is that you have courage, are open, and you want to learn."

In Mack's office, Mack said, "What can I do? I understand my impact, but I need techniques to change." Dave gave the following counsel:

Sy said that you go on too long and when he has had enough, he starts getting irritated. After you've talked a little bit, check with him. Help him stop you. Others have said "you overpower me." Well, after a burst of your feeling, stop and ask for others to come back at you. Ask them whether you have come on too strong. Ask third persons to react. Give the other guy support.

I've observed that you don't usually give a guy a handle. A guy challenges you. You come back at him, but very often you don't meet his point. It leaves a guy feeling helpless. Stop and ask yourself out loud: "Now, am I joining the issue?" Invite him to help you answer your own question.

Mack and Dave discussed these suggestions until Mack was satisfied that he understood what Dave was trying to say.

In departing, Dave said to Mack: "I like you. I like your passion. I'm somewhat the same way. I mean it's hard for me to come to Indianapolis just to maintain a relationship, but if there's a crisis, it's easy to do it and invest myself."

In his discussion with the personnel manager, Dave urged him to take third party roles, cautioning him that, as a member of the staff, he takes additional risks for himself.

The director indicated that he thought "the work" the third-party consultant had facilitated had been "terribly important."

FURTHER DEVELOPMENTS: EVENTUALLY AN IMPROVEMENT

Over the next six weeks following his visit to Indianapolis, Dave received a series of long-distance telephone calls from members of the staff group. These lengthy phone conversations kept Dave informed about developments. They were also opportunities for the callers to air their views, to test their perceptions of the situation against those of Dave, and to elicit Dave's reaction to some interpersonal initiative they had shown, etc.

Dave learned from the personnel manager, the director, and Mack that Sy and Mack were not actively working to inprove their relationship.

Instead, Mack had concluded that his real conflict was with the director. Mack and the director were now seriously working on their conflict in an effort to reach a better understanding.

Mack mentioned several things which seemed to be related to why he hadn't pursued his differences with Sy. (a) He observed that the less he talked in meetings, the more Sy talked, as if Sy was simply relieved to have Mack withdraw, and "to have the show to himself." (b) Mack reported being rebuffed by Sy twice, once regarding a task contribution and the second time in a more interpersonal context. (c) Mack said he now realized that Sy, as assistant director, was only doing what the director wanted, anyway. It was the director, not Sy himself, who decided that Sy would take over the X-Mill project which Mack was so disappointed to lose. In analyzing the situation, Dave made still other inferences: (d) Perhaps Mack decided to work through to establish a relationship with the director because it was the more crucial for his career. (e) Apparently Mack clearly resented what he regarded as the director's close supervisory style; and the director, in turn, had been threatened by Mack's aggressive style. (f) The director, himself, had a tendency to try to work on his *own* relationships with his subordinates, rather than on their relationships with each other.

RECONCILIATION

The consultant made a return visit to the division about six weeks later. He talked with both Sy and Mack individually. Sy stated that he had not gotten together with Mack because he had been so busy with the X-Mill project. He also admitted that he avoided Mack because of the discomfort he experienced in dealing with him. Nevertheless, he indicated an interest in meeting with him and Dave during Dave's two-day visit.

Mack explained to Dave that as a result of the feedback he had received first from Sy and then from the director he had tried to adjust his style of working. He discussed with Dave the nature of these adjustments and the associated personal costs. He wanted to meet with Sy, if the latter was interested.

The three of them went for lunch. Initially, Dave was not sure what use Sy and Mack would want to make of this meeting. It soon became evident that both wanted to deal with their mutual relationship and other matters of personal significance.

Mack began talking about his internal dilemmas, how he had coped with them, the personal costs involved for him, his willingness to suffer his problem, and the career choices which might be approaching—most of which he had not shared with others on the staff. Specifically Mack shared the following inner thoughts:

He had developed a staff concept which helped him resist his tendency to be domineering. He was desperately trying to live up to the model. First, he wanted to learn how to increase others' alternatives, to present issues in a way which did not prejudice them, and to avoid imposing his own views. This was terribly unnatural for him, but it seemed to be what people wanted from him and it appeared to be the company pattern.

Second, he was determined not to inject himself into situations unless someone consulted him or invited him. He didn't believe that he was invited to participate very frequently. This tended to confirm his notion that others, including Sy, were relieved to have him off their backs. He felt underappreciated and rejected. As unsatisfactory as this was for him personally, he believed that this staff pattern was better for the manager group as a whole.

Third, he expressed genuine interest in the welfare and task performance of others, and especially for Sy's work on the X-Mill project.

Mack then described how he was currently coping with the mismatch between others' expectations of him and his own personal needs. In struggling against his natural tendency to completely and enthusiastically invest himself in a job—probably more thoroughly than most managers—he was attempting to make an adequate, but measured investment in the controller's job. This also involved fighting his second tendency to completely withdraw—a matter of central significance in his relationship with Sy.

Mack finally talked about his personal career alternatives. The net personal cost for him to live by the staff concept was great and he was pursuing other job possibilities. He had come to the conclusion that he was effective as a promoter—a one-man show. He could get along with superiors and subordinates, but not peers. Maybe he would find a job where peer relations were not important.

Dave had learned some of these feelings and thoughts from his earlier discussion with Mack. Therefore, he could both encourage and assist Mack in verbalizing his feelings. Sy was silent throughout and did not make a verbal response when Mack had finished. Dave's own observations convinced him that Sy had been listening empathically to Mack and was moved. Mack, however, had revealed feelings, thoughts, explanations, and prospects that were of personal significance. Colloquially, he had "spilled his guts." Now he appeared to be anxious about Sy's response—or the lack of a specific response.

Dave asked Sy to share his current feelings and thoughts—to respond to Mack. Sy expressed feelings of understanding and compassion for Mack and sincere appreciation of Mack's concern for Sy's welfare, in particular Sy's development in the X-Mill project. He also recognized Mack's interest in being directly helpful to him. He acknowledged that Mack was accurate in his perception that he (Sy) preferred a "middle-of-the-road" type of staff pattern. Sy said he could neither cope with Mack when the latter was at full throttle, nor accept him when he withdrew completely.

Sy continued to talk thoughtfully. He said "I find I do prefer to deal with (a subordinate of Mack's) on controller matters rather than with you." Mack's response was, "Beautiful!" The exclamation was spontaneous and vigorous, as if the authenticity of Sy's remark about his preference to work with Mack's subordinate was necessary to make Sy's earlier statement of compassion and understanding for Mack fully credible. Dave was also struck by the combination of sympathy and toughness in Sy's overall response to Mack's revelations of his internal dilemmas. Mack went on to request Sy's support for a promotion he was seeking for the subordinate in question. The promotion to assistant controller would ensure that he would be Mack's successor.

The long encounter over lunch was a very emotional experience—a type of reconciliation between Sy and Mack. They had experienced an emotionally moving self-disclosure, reciprocated by an expression of deeply felt concern. This was in contrast with the basic antagonism expressed in the earlier confrontation. They had now expressed mutual respect and concern for one another's welfare. While their respective styles kept them from wanting to work with each other, their negative feelings had been replaced by a form of positive feelings. Dave's prediction was that they might yet be able to develop a working relationship.

The third-party consultant was the instigator of the opportunity for dialogue in this second explicit attempt to work on the relationship. He was relatively less active than in the earlier confrontation encounter, but his presence had clearly provided the impetus and the reassurance necessary for the principals to meet again. The mutual interest in pursuing the relationship had apparently remained, but had not been acted upon, presumably because Sy had not been confident that he and Mack could work on it by themselves.

The Outcome and Conclusion

Within the next few weeks, Mack and the director worked through their differences and reached a mutually satisfying and productive relationship. When the consultant visited two months later, Mack had developed a pattern of working with peers in the organization and an outlook on life and work with which he was quite pleased. Finally, the consultant also observed two long business appraisal and planning meetings in which Sy and Mack worked intensively with each other—and they worked effectively.

Thus over the four-month period covered by this case study, the relationship between Sy and Mack had improved markedly. In the beginning it was negative on two counts: it greatly interfered with their current work; and it was a liability in terms of future career prospects. At the end of the period, the relationship was satisfactory (not exceptional) on both counts.

The series of encounters reported here, in which the third party played a central role, were evidently instrumental in producing this change. During the period between the confrontation and reconciliation encounters, there were changes affecting Mack individually, which also created the potential for a change in the relationship. However, the principals did not really work together by themselves, and certainly did not make progress on their relationship. If anything, Mack had become discouraged by the failure of his minor attempts to resume a dialogue on their relationship.

As it turned out, the burden of behavior change had fallen on Mack. He had formulated his choice as "adapt somewhat or leave"—and neither was easy for him. Dave, concerned about the personal costs which Mack might incur in foregoing his assertiveness, had provided support for his search for a new position. A modest search effort had not produced a satisfactory alternative for Mack and his family. Moreover, Mack had a positive interest in developing an ability to work effectively with peers, even if that involved throttling this aggressiveness. It should be reported that Mack's change was not absolute. Later he was able to resume his aggressiveness in ways that did not interfere with the functioning of others. Within two years both men were promoted—to positions elsewhere in the firm.

4

FRED–CHARLES: SEARCHING FOR
AN ACCOMMODATION

This chapter reports an episode between the personnel manager and the production superintendent of a division of a large medical supply firm. A significant aspect of their confrontation involved clarifying their differences in an effort to find more accommodating interpersonal and staff-line relationships. The third party's interventions during this confrontation were of a much more active variety than those in the two preceding cases. In order to focus on these active interventions, the format of this chapter will differ from the earlier chapters. It will present background material and a running account of much of the confrontation. However, other detailed material about the episode will be introduced within the framework of an analysis of third-party interventions.

BACKGROUND TO THE CONFRONTATION
BETWEEN CHARLES AND FRED

Charles, personnel manager, and Fred, production superintendent, both reported directly to the division's general manager and were members of his staff. (See Fig. 4–1.) Dave, who participated in the conflict episode as a third party, had worked as a consultant to the general manager's staff one or two days every other month over the past few years.

Sources of Stress on the Principals

About six months earlier, Charles had moved to his present job from a position of lesser responsibility in another division of the corporation. Thus far, his performance had not met the expectations of the general manager. The general manager and an official from Corporate Personnel had discussed the matter with him. In brief, Charles was under considerable pressure from his superiors to prove himself.

One specific criticism was that Charles was not functioning as a human relations and organizational counselor to the general manager and other members of the staff. The previous personnel manager had given this function considerable attention and had done an effective job. The general manager himself had expressed a need for more assistance of this type from Charles; also, other interpersonal and organizational issues were causing difficulty within the staff. Charles, for his part, considered this function less important than certain other personnel functions which, in his opinion, had been neglected by his predecessor.

Secondly, Charles was criticized for his handling of union-management relations. Specifically, the general manager believed that Charles was unnecessarily hostile and suspicious toward the union. Division managers were proud of the accommodative relationship that they had developed with the union president, who they believed was reasonably responsible and trustworthy. Charles had not been directly responsible for labor relations in his previous job; nevertheless, he had been in a personnel department where the relations with the union had been very antagonistic, an experience which probably influenced his current attitude.

Fred had been promoted recently to the position of production superintendent. While a few persons with whom he had worked had experienced difficulty in getting along with him, he also was highly regarded by other associates and generally had the confidence of the general manager. The production superintendent was assumed to be progressing well in getting on top of his job and coping with the constant pressure to solve new problems and improve performance. Of the two principals in this case, Fred enjoyed relatively more organizational support.

Job Interdependence. Their organizational relationship was an important one. Although both were interested in improving their relationship, their

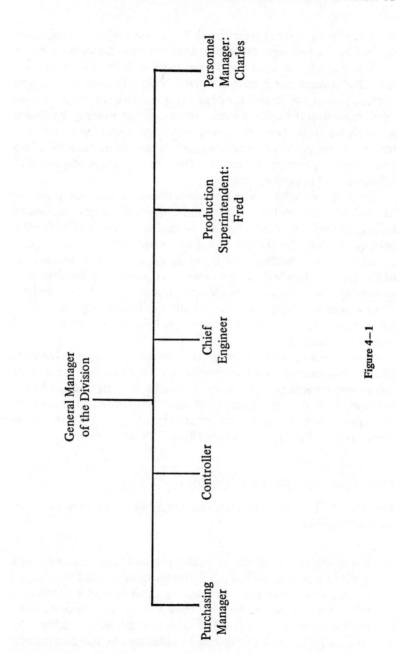

Figure 4–1

sense of urgency was not symmetrical. By far, the majority of employees serviced by the personnel department were in the production organization headed by Fred. The nature of the personnel work to be done was such that Charles could not operate effectively if he and his department were not accepted by Fred and his department. In fact, Fred's prior close relationship with the union president made it almost necessary for Charles to develop a satisfactory relationship with Fred in order to develop one with the union president. In contrast, only a fraction of the work of the production department depended upon the personnel department's efforts—at least in the short run.

Because they were new to the general manager's staff, both principals had had relatively limited contact with Dave before the episode reported here. They were aware that Dave had worked as a third party with other pairs on the staff. Charles himself had been present, but not a participant, in one case. He understood what Dave was trying to do, knew about some of the types of functions he performed, and presumably had developed trust in him and confidence in his competence. Fred had had only brief direct exposure to Dave, but he apparently was reassured by the fact that several close colleagues and two superiors had placed their confidence and trust in the consultant.

One common practice of members of the staff was to phone Dave and discuss organizational and interpersonal matters when they arose—using the phone conversation to clarify their own thinking and get Dave's reactions. Both Fred and Charles had taken the initiative to phone Dave and discuss their interpersonal conflict. Thus, Dave had learned of the intensifying conflict two weeks before his visit to the division.

Fred's Views of the Developing Conflict

Late on a Friday afternoon Dave received a phone call from Fred who reported the following:

> I'm calling you about my relationship with Charles, especially as a result of a meeting we had today. Our relationship is not what it's got to be. I don't know what the trouble is . . . it exposes itself when we ask how we can use his service. I think he doesn't trust me, the way I run my department. I've tried to share this with him . . . he feels I've rejected his offer of service and I can see how he might construe it that way.

Today we were talking about a fifth-step grievance. It concerned absenteeism, where we in production admittedly have done a poor job. So what he comes up with is, "Well, you know, I've offered help five times and you haven't taken us up on it." I said, "Crap, that's an oversimplification." I acknowledged the truth, but resented the patness of his answer. Tied in with this is a hidden gripe, which is that I'm running the department five men short, in part because Personnel has not gotten me the men. Therefore, I'm annoyed at getting pat answers.

The fact is that we have not placed priority on absenteeism versus some other pressing problems. But he (Charles) sits in a comfortable position, where he can't do anything wrong. It's easy for him to throw darts.

I told him, "Yes, we should have invited you in, but your hands are not so clean, you share in this; I resent the excessive criticism." We need to sit down and work on this.

Dave asked Fred how he felt now about this interchange with Charles. Fred replied,

I shared so much that I'm embarrassed. The meeting included the general manager, the chief engineer, and one of Charles' subordinates. I'm sorry about Charles' subordinates being there. They all remained more objective than Charles and I.

Dave asked Fred whether he and Charles had disagreed on how to handle the grievance.

Yes, that's an issue. He was very suspicious of the union president and wanted to hold back on something the rest of us thought was fair to do.

As a matter of fact, I, too, locked horns with the union president initially when he took over. At first, he saw things as black and white; but now he sees them as grey, and we have developed trust in each other.

In any event, when Charles came here, I had been sharing things with the union president. Charles said he thought that something I'd just done had been unwise, that it might lead to a side agreement. Well, I blew my stack and blasted him, because I have better judgment than that, and I trust my subordinates to have better judgment than that.

As it turns out, I see Charles going through some of the same things with the union president that I did. I just hope he works through to an understanding. The union president came to me and we talked about this grievance. I related this conversation to Charles and said that he should take the union president at his word.

Dave commented that it seemed "pretty understandable" that Charles would resent somewhat the close relationship between Fred and the union president. Fred answered:

That's true, but if he doesn't trust me, I'm teed off.

Also, shortly after he arrived, there was a salary meeting in which he (Charles) talked in circles. I didn't think he could talk straight, but now I believe he can do better than he did at that time.

The question is why doesn't he trust me? But when I put it on the table that way, he says, "What makes you believe that?"

It bothers me, it grinds me, that he can get to me so quickly. Not that he tries to. I don't have that kind of relationship with anyone else here ... I ought to be able to be cool and philosophical. There is no personal animosity. He's a nice wholesome guy ... a regular fellow ... nothing personal involved ... we don't socialize outside business.

Dave asked Fred to think out loud about the ways in which his own relationship with the union president might be a factor in Charles' attitude. Fred responded:

As I went into the grievance meeting, I said, "I agree with the union president." When Charles challenged my ability to predict what the union would do, I also said, "I've got the best relationship with the union president ... I think I can feel him out before the meeting." Charles' response was that any meeting before the fifth step might dilute the fifth step. I answered "I've already met him." ... Yes, this could be threatening to Charles. However, the union president wants to develop a good relationship with the personnel manager as well as with the production superintendent.

Charles' Views

The following Wednesday, Dave received a phone call from Charles who reported the following:

I had an emotional meeting with Fred last Friday. It resulted from my strong concern with absenteeism and tardiness. A few months ago I had identified a mounting cost problem. I had said to Fred, "Hey, who is worrying about this?" Fred answered, "I'll have my two production supervisors go to work on it." I said, "Can I help?" He said, "No." Two weeks later I asked how it was going, and again he reassured me. This happened three more times. Finally we had a grievance, which I think could have been avoided. A supervisor cracked down too hard without tightening up in advance—gradually and with warnings.

Monday morning I talked with Fred, identifying our conflict. It may not be more important than a working relationship. I felt the pressing need to go to work on the absenteeism problem. I said, "I didn't want to undercut your position by working with your men without your permission." He said, "Go ahead and work on the problems you see." Therefore, I believe it's at least partly resolved.

Maybe (the chief engineer) has talked with him, urging him not to simply get the bit in his teeth and go charging off without worrying about implications for others.

I had a warm feeling for (the chief engineer) on Saturday morning. He said, "Let me know if I can help. I like both of you too well to let you guys get into trouble with each other."

I believe there is a fringe benefit of my confrontation with Fred, because it took place with (the general manager and the chief engineer) present. I hope the general manager, especially, can see me other than reserved. This incident revealed my willingness to take some risks, which he has been urging me to do.

Immediately before the confrontation in the meeting with Dave, Charles told Dave that at least three others had had trouble in trying to work with Fred at one point or another, indicating that he was reassured it was not simply his (Charles') problem.

The Principals' Relationships with other Staff Members

In addition to having the above background information, Dave sketched out in his own mind the relevant sociometry of the members of the staff as he perceived it. (See Fig. 4–2.) This analysis confirmed for Dave that the

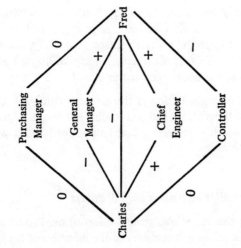

Figure 4–2. Relationship of Staff Members with Fred and Charles

Key
+ indicates a positive mutual trust relationship
- indicates a low trust relationship
0 denotes an indifferent or ambivalent relationship

chief engineer was the only staff member who had positive relations with both principals and might serve as an internal third party.

An Illustrative Conflict

The consultant spent the first half day of a two-day visit to the division observing and assisting in the critique of the general manager's staff meeting. The following interchange occurred between Fred and Charles. The latter suggested that a management decision on hours and scheduling might involve certain labor relations risks—either a union charge of a lockout, or a vigorous attempt in the next negotiations to get a contract provision restricting management's flexibility.

Fred (referring to Charles' concerns): That is a very judgmental thing. I intend to lobby to the very bitter end not to run that premium overtime shift.

The general manager (interjecting): I know it is a matter of judgment and I don't know how to weigh the risk, but it should be considered ... can I hear from you and Charles on this? (The implication was that he wanted them to get together outside of staff meeting and then report to him.)

Fred (continuing to pursue the matter, implying that the decision was an instance of a more general issue): I think we ought to make this decision by the numbers. We can't give here and there. The point is we need to run this plant as it should be run.

Charles (retorting): Bear in mind that the worst thing that could happen by running by the numbers is a lockout. There are some potential problems from a labor relations point of view. Let me dig into this.

The general manager: Both of you dig into this.

The boss attempted to ensure that the two would meet, discuss the matter, and report to him. Also, he achieved some neutrality *vis à vis* the principals by first urging Fred to consider Charles' views, and then by prompting Charles not to go off on his own. The interchange added the boss' pressure on the parties to work on their relationship, and provided a tangible issue to use as a vehicle.

Decision to Work on the Charles–Fred Conflict

Dave had avoided any decision in advance of the staff meeting about how his time would be used over the next day and a half. Several individual staff members had expressed an interest in spending time with him, in some cases alone, in other cases paired with a member of the staff, and in still other cases with one or more subordinates. Dave wanted to resist trying to respond to more than a few of these, and he wanted the choices to be made in the staff group context. He also wanted to make it clear that he felt they were free to replan on the basis of developments.

His own preferred method for working during this visit was to work with relationship pairs, where both persons were staff members. He knew that there were several interpersonal differences among staff members which were affecting current organizational performance, were psychologically stressful for the persons involved, and could have direct implications for their careers if the conflicts were not resolved. Moreover, even if in these respects there were equally important interpersonal conflicts involving persons not on the staff, Dave would have preferred to work with staff members, because he already had background information, including his observations of them in staff meetings, and because he could better ensure that both parties were participants to the decision to meet with the consultant.

The consultant's criteria for preferring to focus on one interpersonal staff conflict rather than another included: Do both persons seem relatively equally interested in getting together with the consultant? Which pair seems most anxious to meet? Which pair's expression of interest does the group as a whole seem to support most? Where does he, as a consultant, feel he has the most understanding?

At the end of the staff meeting, the staff participated in a critique of their meeting. During the critique, several interpersonal difficulties were identified and briefly discussed. Then Dave asked group members to consider how he should plan to use the next day and a half. This allowed for the generation of the kind of information relevant to the above criteria.

The general plan which emerged was for Dave to meet with others during lunch and immediately after lunch, and then get together with Charles and Fred about 3.30 p.m. That meeting "could run over into dinner, if necessary." This open-ended arrangement was probably the most conducive to a good dialogue and confrontation between Charles and Fred. It was also planned for the consultant to participate in a task group's meetings on the following day.

Of what significance to the Fred–Charles confrontation itself was the above manner in which it was planned? Some possibilities can be suggested. Each member of the pair was given an explicit opportunity to express his interest, or lack of interest, in meeting. If he was reluctant to meet, it was possible to signal this in a variety of subtle ways (e.g., by holding back, by finding it difficult to agree upon a meeting time, by sidetracking the discussion). Also, the discussion leading to this decision showed this particular pair the extent to which other staff members gave priority to the improvement of their interpersonal differences. The public commitment to work on the relationship may have increased motivation to work through their differences, or at least to manage them better.

CONFRONTATION: DIFFERENTIATION PHASE

Getting the Issue on the Table

The session was started by Dave suggesting that Fred and Charles continue their discussion of the disagreement raised during the staff meeting earlier that day. They agreed, and proceeded to do so. Thus the third party could observe their pattern of interaction, hear their stated positions, and listen for their underlying concerns before he needed to make a more active intervention.

As the discussion proceeded, it became clear that Charles was not necessarily opposed to the decision urged by Fred. He was asking to "reserve judgment" until he had an opportunity to get the advice of a lawyer and corporate personnel. The decision would be delayed a day or two until he had the primary advice he needed in order to represent the labor-relations view. Fred, on the other hand, felt that such a posture was unduly cautious, asserting that even a production manager like himself could see that the decision obviously would *not* have the labor-relations implications Charles was alluding to. He saw no reason why the scheduling decision couldn't be made "tentatively," and then, if Charles learned something which made him believe the decision was unwise, it could be discussed. Inasmuch as the decision affected schedules three weeks hence, and Charles could get his advice within a couple of days, there were no urgent *action* implications of the issue. Nevertheless, the disagreement appeared to be relevant to their general interpersonal and staff-line conflict.

After some time, and just as the discussion-debate appeared to have become repetitive, Dave attempted to shift their attention to the more general form of the issue. He asked:

> Is this specific decision just an occasion for you to work on your differing views about the role of the personnel manager? I see you, Charles, using this to make the point that whenever there might be

labor-relations implications you believe you should be consulted, and that Fred should not rely upon his own unilateral judgment about the importance of potential labor-relations implications. Am I right that you feel you have trouble with Personnel being ignored along these lines?

Turning to Fred, Dave continued,

Fred, I see you saying that the decision is obvious and that you are annoyed with Charles for making a jurisdictional issue out of it. If that is correct, is it a common pattern?

The discussion which followed confirmed that these were significant themes in their disagreements.

Identifying Stylistic Differences

Then, somewhat later, Fred noted that he and Charles were very different. Picking up this idea, Dave suggested that each share his views of how their personal styles differed. During the discussion which followed, Fred and Charles displayed the contrasts set forth in Fig. 4–3.

After both had revealed their perceptions, Fred added another difference: he saw himself as taking people and issues at face value, whereas Charles was "probing, distrustful, doubtful, assuming a credibility gap, conjuring up problems . . . " Fred had become more emotional as he identified additional perceptions of Charles. From time to time, at Dave's urging, he had shared the type of feelings he experienced as a result of Charles' style; he felt himself "seething," "ground," "strained to the limit." Fred also believed that Charles got "bothered" and "bent out of shape" in reaction to him. Fred had been allowed to predominate in this discussion because he appeared to have relatively greater need to get these types of interpersonal perceptions out on the table.

In turning to hear more from Charles, Dave reviewed as completely as possible all of Fred's perceptions of him, enabling Charles to respond to an issue which was relatively important to him, rather than simply the most recent one mentioned by Fred.

Charles objected to Fred's charge that he tended to be distrustful toward others, saying that Fred could never give him specific instances. Thereupon, Fred related the fifth-step grievance episode and asserted that Charles' approach to the union reflected unduly low trust. It developed

Fred saw himself as:
    Direct

    Dealing in "black and white"

    Shirt sleeves, stevedore

    Relying upon personal
    relationships

    Decisive

    "Laying matters on the
    table to look at them"

Charles saw Fred as:
    Impulsive

    Not thorough

    Not caring whom he made
    problems for; not considering
    his effect on others

Fred saw Charles as:
    Indirect, using hidden meanings,
    meandering, hypothetical

    Treating everything as "grey"

    Scholarly, professional, cap
    and gown

    Insisting upon formal
    organizational channels

    Indecisive, hesitant, cautious,
    "Sorting things out into
    separate piles"

Charles saw himself as:
    Looking ahead

    Thorough

    More considerate

Figure 4–3.

that the two disagreed completely in their recollection of these events essential to Fred's point.

During this discussion, the consultant noted a pattern in Charles' behavior which appeared to irritate Fred and add to his tension. It was also irritating to Dave. Charles had a tendency to ask a leading question which either forced an admission of fault, or revealed inconsistencies. It was a prosecution or examining style. Over the next hour, Dave made four types of interventions to call attention to this pattern and either modify it, or nullify its adverse effects.

First, Dave called attention to the cross-examination style and tested Fred for how he was reacting to it. Fred confirmed his resentment. Thus, Charles had more information about how others react to this pattern of his.

Second, and in connection with the above intervention, Dave shared what his *own* reaction to this style would be, if he were the person being cross-examined. He used a hostile, graphic gesture.

Third, at a later point, Dave stopped the continuing attempt to reconstruct what had happened at the fifth-step meeting (where there were very contradictory recollections of events), and asked "What would each of you be inclined to do with this difference?" Their responses dramatically illustrated one of their differences: Fred was inclined to drop it as not being productive. Charles was inclined to get a witness, cross-examine him, and take any step required in order to determine who was correct. When Charles reflected upon this difference, he gained some insight into his own pattern which he acknowledged might not always be productive.

Then Charles, who had had less opportunity to state what he didn't like about Fred, added an item.

Charles: Fred, you lack humility.

Fred: And you want to teach it to me?

Dave: Charles, do you see *yourself* as having humility?

Charles: Yes.

Dave: Fred, do you see Charles that way?

Fred: It's *false* humility.

Charles then cited his earlier admission that he lacked the knowledge to make a judgment on the labor-relations implications of the scheduling issue. He indicated that this was humility. Fred disagreed with that interpretation. He observed that this "admission of lack of knowledge" was tactical to Charles' purposes and didn't strike him as humility.

Later, Fred sharpened one source of resentment toward Charles. He saw Charles as doubting the judgment of production management on labor relations matters, and acting as if he were "saving production people from their own transgressions," as if he were "standing at the pass."

Escalation of Personal Attacks

Still later in the discussion, one of the two principals referred to a recent interchange between them. Fred had observed that the price of cartons of milk in the canteen had been increased from 15¢ to 20¢. He had recalled that the profits from the canteen went to the recreation fund, which apparently had more money than it could spend. Therefore, he had mentioned his disapproval of the price increase to a member of Personnel (either Charles or a subordinate). The two principals began rehashing the experience and using the instance to support their respective perceptions of each other. Their dialogue escalated in tone and included the following comments:

Charles: My subordinates said to me, "Boy, are we in bad shape if our production superintendent doesn't have anything better to do than second guess us on the price of milk."

Fred: That's defensive. It's not clear you had a good reason. The price of milk affects everyone. Only a few benefit from the recreation fund.

Charles: You are being defensive. You are the only one in the plant who has complained about the price of milk. What does that tell you?

Fred: Somebody has to speak up. For example, to cite another instance, if I hadn't called your attention to the bad trash situation people would still be stepping over it day after day. It's funny, the cafeteria is the only thing you have to manage. (Fred was making the point that unlike the personnel department, Production continuously has to make decisions and take action, and therefore becomes vulnerable to criticism. This asymmetry had been a source of discomfort to Fred. Here, in the milk incident, he appeared to be trying to achieve more symmetry in this respect.)

Charles: If you would like to run the cafeteria, we'd be happy to let you take it.

Dave cut off the discussion at this point. He indicated that it was 6:15 p.m. and that the chief engineer who was to join them for drinks had expected them to come by his office about half an hour earlier. Although Dave did not formulate it in his mind at the time, another reason favoring the termination of the discussion when he did was that it had escalated (or degenerated) into more personal attacks, which seemed to intensify the mutual antagonism, rather than clarify basic issues.

Partly in order to provide some closure on the discussion, he summarized the "essential point" of each of the principals, and indicated that each had an understandable view:

> The discussion of the milk incident has been somewhat repetitive. Let me try to state the points each of you are making, as I hear them. Fred is saying, "Why should you get upset if I bring to your attention the idea that it doesn't make sense to increase the price of milk when the funds aren't all being spent now." He is saying to you, Charles, "Can't you accept this idea on its merit?" I believe I can understand Fred's sentiment here.

> On the other hand, Charles is saying to you, Fred, "This criticism is symbolic of your attitude toward us, of your tendency to get involved in our area, and we resent it. It's as if you *wanted* to find fault—and it's this general attitude that bothers us." That, too, I must admit, is an understandable view.

> Am I right? That is, did I capture your essential points? (Both agreed.)

Apparently such a summary statement by the third party increased their respective feelings of being understood, and also avoided the question of which of them was going to have the last word in that interchange. In addition, Dave overlooked the more personal and more destructive attacks and counterattacks which both had exchanged in tactical support of stating and supporting their "essential points." It might have been more helpful for Dave to have noted these tactics and helped the parties to understand how this type of interchange had developed or degenerated. This might have been an excellent way for Dave to differentiate between the types of confrontation which he believed constructive and which he was trying to promote, and the type of conflict interchange which he believed was counterproductive. This opportunity was clear to him only on hindsight.

CONTINUING THE DIALOGUE FOR NEW INSIGHTS

The chief engineer joined the three men, and they all went to a restaurant lounge for drinks and later to the dining room for dinner. The group continued to work until 11:30 p.m.

The chief engineer had joined the group at the consultant's invitation and with the concurrence of Charles and Fred. Although he was relatively inactive, he made two important specific interventions and performed some passive but important functions for the confrontation. First, he asked the group to help him think through a specific decision he had to make concerning a subordinate of his, to which the group responded and discussed this with him for about an hour. Second, when asked at one point for his reactions to what was going on between Fred and Charles, he gave them a common, blunt reaction, namely, "I think you guys are presently both lecturing each other." After that comment, they both dug in and dealt with each other more directly. Third, the more passive functions of his presence included such things as (a) limiting any tendencies of the principals to use "unfair" tactics; (b) providing the prospect of additional forward continuity of the dialogue by being available to them, either individually or as a pair.

The following material departs from the format of providing a running account of the conflict, but wherever possible, takes up elements of the interaction in the order in which they occurred. The discussion focuses on the consultant's interventions, first describing the intervention in an abstract way, and then illustrating it.

ANALYZING THE ONGOING PROCESS

An interesting interchange illustrates the power of analyzing the ongoing interaction. Fred, the production superintendent, turned to Dave after a lull in the discussions.

Fred: Dave, it's a little off the current subject, but I want to get your reaction to an idea. I've been talking with the union president about what you've been doing with the management staff and he is intrigued and interested. You know he likes to develop his own abilities ... I was wondering what your ideas are about spending an hour or so with him?

Dave: By posing that question to me, you've created a dilemma for me. It's an interesting idea and I do want to respond to it, but, if I do, we will have created additional problems in your relationship with Charles. Have you checked the idea with Charles? (Fred indicated he had not.) My guess is that right now he's sitting here feeling excluded, bypassed, and is getting riled up. This is an instance when you are not recognizing him as the personnel manager.

Fred: My gosh, I see what you mean. It was unconscious. It never occurred to me I was excluding or bypassing Charles.

Making it Difficult for One to Dismiss Another's Perceptions

Dave used a person's own language or reasoning to persuade him to take something seriously (e.g., to prevent his discounting a piece of threatening information which had been introduced). For example, early in the episode, Fred reported an instance in which Charles had been suspicious of others. He generalized from the instance by referring to it as just a "pebble on the path"; he was asserting that it was merely a part of a pattern, that he could cite other examples. Later, when Fred would slightly ignore, evade, dispute, or depreciate the personnel area (in trivial or accidental ways, in and of themselves), Dave would acknowledge that such an instance taken by itself should not be cause for so much reaction as it elicited from Charles, but that when it was viewed as a part of a pattern, "a pebble on the path," Charles' reactions became less surprising.

Gaining a Differentiated View of the Other Person

Dave called attention to what he perceived as important variations in a person's behavior during the period of their discussions. Then he would check with the second person to see whether he perceived the same variations. In some cases, one type of behavior had been negatively reacted to, and the other behavior had been positively received. Dave would press to achieve as much of this type of differentiation as possible. An illustration follows.

Recall that earlier in the dialogue Fred had said that Charles showed "a false humility." He had said that when Charles admitted he didn't know something, the admission was tactical (e.g., to buy time). Later in the day, there was an instance where Charles was "piling on," was showing "delight" at the fact that Fred had been brought up short by one of the consultant's observations. Dave turned to Charles and confronted him with the idea that he had just "piled on." Charles fully appreciated the point. His face flushed with shame and he said, "I'm sorry ..." "I regret that ... I don't like that (in myself)." However, Fred appeared to completely ignore these statements of regret or sentiments of shame expressed by Charles.

Since Dave believed there had been something very different about Charles' expression of humility in these two instances, he confronted Fred, and said, "I want to check something out with you. What did Charles just say and was it another instance of 'false humility'?" Fred said that he did *not* feel it was false in this instance. In effect, Dave gave maximum opportunity for Fred to reinforce Charles' behavior in the second instance. More importantly, the intervention acknowledged to Charles that he was perceived in one way one time and in another a second time.

The Parties' Expectations

The consultant counseled the parties to anticipate disappointments in the course of trying to build a relationship. Consider the following interchange:

Charles: At some point the whole thing will click. I feel we will have an excellent relationship. (This was said in an enthusiastic way.)

Fred: It's not that easy. I see it as a process of being open about how we interfere with and grind each other, and gradually being more accommodative.

Dave: I guess I see it much as Fred does. In part, it's because guys like you, Charles, generally find it easier to get along with guys like Fred than vice versa. (Dave referred to their interpersonal patterns.)

Dave also pointed out the rejection potential for Charles in the foregoing. Charles acknowledged that he had felt immediate rejection. The parties were alerted to this problem of rejection. They discussed whether it was possible to take the sting out of future "overtures not reciprocated." As a result of this interchange, Charles might in the future be more likely to talk directly with Fred about the effect of such rejection, rather than to counter-attack in an indirect way.

Similarities between the Principals

The consultant identified similarities between the parties, especially as they referred to instances occurring in the interaction (e.g., the patterns of lecturing, scolding, preaching, condescending, helping or informing). The following illustrates the point:

Fred had effectively made a point of Charles' lecturing, pointing out that, not only did he see Charles this way, but his subordinates did too.

Fred had said, "You act as if it's your job to point out mistakes, how people went wrong, but not to work to prevent problems in advance."

Much later the chief engineer said, "You're both lecturing each other." Dave agreed and pointed out to Fred that he usually preceded a lecturing bit with the words, "You see . . ." Dave provided several illustrations from the past hour. Fred fully registered the feedback and said he hadn't even realized that he was using the words "You see."

Common Goals

Dave identified a future common goal where they might really go astray if they hadn't worked things out by then: resolving management's priorities on items in labor negotiations. This and other third-party interventions are illustrated by the following interchange:

Fred: I want to make sure my two subordinates have a say about the items that go forward to the corporate office.

Charles: I intend to provide that opportunity.

Fred: (Made a very divisive, challenging statement about the amount of control he wanted for line versus staff.)

Charles: (Made a statement to the effect that the line would have influence, but would not have final say.)

Fred: (Referred to "unanimity.")

Charles: It's unrealistic to state in advance that all of the decisions will be unanimous.

Fred: Well, perhaps this has become hypothetical.

Dave: Yes, but why? I see you in this instance as feisty; as if you were looking for ways to challenge Personnel, especially Charles . . . I'm afraid that unless you guys have worked this through, the management discussions prior to labor negotiations are going to involve more conflict than the negotiations themselves . . . An initial difference of opinion will become exaggerated and polarized. (Then, turning to the chief engineer.) I rather hope you get involved—as a sort of neutral guy—in these preliminary discussions.

Charles (chiming in): That's why *I* said I wanted you involved.

Dave (glowering at Charles): There's a difference in what I said and what you said. I saw him (the chief engineer) as a neutral. I see you as making a bid for a coalition, or for using my statement against Fred.

The above interchange illustrates several other third-party interventions. First, Dave identified the chief engineer as a third party, legitimating his behavior in this role, and coordinating expectations for him to play this role in a particular future situation. Second, Dave disassociated himself from, and "punished" Charles for, an act which appeared to have the intent of putting Fred down.

OUTCOMES FROM THE CONFRONTATION

What were the prospects for resolving the substantive and emotional conflicts in the Fred–Charles case? Their respective role expectations did involve substantial disagreement; however, these differences presumably could be partly compromised and partly integrated, provided the two could develop some positive interpersonal rapport.

During the six months they had known each other, their encounters had been only moderately intensive; the resultant interpersonal resentments were genuine, but did not appear to be so strong that they could not be worked through. Finally, while their personal styles (indirectness, impulsivity) might be expected to be the basis of irritation, they did not seem to be significant enough to prevent interpersonal accommodation.

In conclusion, the conflict appeared to be amenable to resolution or better control. If the differences in their respective labor-relations philosophies and role definitions had been more basic, then dialogue and process interventions of the type described here would have limited potential. In that case, solutions would require change in personnel or organization structure.

If the jurisdictional issue could be worked through, there was the prospect for a creative balance and synthesis of their respective orientations to labor relations and their styles of decision-making. The jurisdictional issue would be less significant if the blaming pattern subsided; the blaming pattern in turn, would be less obtrusive if the two were able to develop mutual respect and trust.

The confrontation which took place was without a high emotional climax; rather it was sustained at a moderate level of emotionality. There were periods in which the discussion became repetitive and circular, but on the whole there was a progressive movement to the interchange. For example, greater insights into one's own or the other's interpersonal patterns and personal concerns were first registered, later illustrated again by subsequent actions, and still later anticipated by one or both of the parties. Having a common understanding of these patterns and being able to anticipate them, they could learn to joke about them and perhaps to avoid the interaction pattern. Therefore, the pattern itself (which was mutually offensive) did not provide "more fuel to the fire."

At the end of the day, each of the parties had more insight into what he was doing to promote the conflict, and each appeared to have *some* increased confidence in the positive intentions of the other. They had a little better understanding of the underlying emotional-organizational bases which were common to most of the substantive issues about which they found themselves in disagreement. It was not, however, apparent that their respect for each other had been greatly increased. They had learned about and practiced some ways of working on their misunderstandings that were probably more productive than those they had used previously. They had a common understanding of the difficulty and the time which would probably be involved in improving their relationship; that is, Charles became less hopeful for a short-run breakthrough, and Fred became more optimistic about eventually developing an accommodative pattern. There probably was higher commitment to improve the relationship and to engage in joint projects such as supervisory training. There was increased awareness of the future costs of not being able to manage their interpersonal conflict, particularly as it could affect preparation for labor negotiations a few months hence.

Both explicitly expressed satisfaction with the process and its results during the meeting. The next day Charles expressed feelings that they had made headway, and yet clearly manifested some continued basic distrust of Fred. Fred, without saying just how his attitude or perceptions of Charles had changed, said that the day had been one of the most significant educational experiences in his life.

The confrontation itself increased the incentive to resolve their differences. First, there was a tendency for each of them to want to justify the time and energy invested in the effort to improve their relationship, and also to meet the expectations of other staff members. Second, the process underscored at least one tangible area of interdependence, namely the approaching labor negotiations.

Although the confrontation had provided a basis and a start for reaching some working accommodation, Charles left the division and the corporation before the full effects of their efforts to build a relationship could be felt. The primary reason for his termination was that he had not gained a relationship of mutual confidence with the general manager.

5

DIAGNOSTIC MODEL OF INTERPERSONAL CONFLICT

Our diagnostic model of interpersonal conflict involves four basic elements—the conflict issues, the circumstances which precipitate manifest conflict, the conflict-relevant acts of the principals, and the various consequences of the conflict. We shall analyze and compare these elements across the case studies presented above; our aim will be to suggest diagnostically useful distinctions. The analysis also asserts the cyclical nature of interpersonal conflict as depicted in Fig. 5-1, and identifies variables which determine whether the cycle is benevolent, malevolent, or self-maintaining. Finally, the discussion enables us to develop and illustrate certain operational objectives of conflict management. Each of four strategies of conflict management relates to a different one of the four basic elements of the cyclical model.

CYCLICAL AND DYNAMIC NATURE OF INTERPERSONAL CONFLICT

Interpersonal conflicts are *cyclical*. Two persons who are opposed are only periodically engaged in manifest conflict. At one point in time the issues between them represent only latent conflict. Then, for some reason, their opposition becomes salient, the parties engage in a set of conflict-relevant

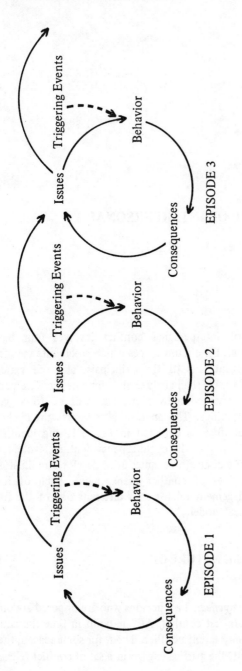

Figure 5-1. A Cyclical Model of Interpersonal Conflict.

behaviors, they experience the consequences of the interchange; and then once again the conflict becomes less salient and less manifest for a time. If the persons remain in interdependence, the manifest conflict will tend to recur at some point.

Interpersonal conflicts also tend to be *dynamic*, that is to say, from one cycle to the next the issues or the form of the manifest conflict will typically undergo change. *Escalation* refers to a tendency for the relationship to become more conflictful. *De-escalation* refers to a trend toward less conflict. For example, as we will analyze below, the number of conflict issues of a recurrent conflict may be continually modified as a function of the tactics and outcome of the conflict interchanges. An increase in the number of issues constitutes one type of escalation; and conversely, a decrease is one form of de-escalation. The above terms refer to the direction of change.

To refer to the purposive efforts to bring about these directional changes, we introduce other concepts. If as a part of an overall strategy of conflict management temporary escalation is desirable, we will speak of acting to *de-control* the conflict. Similarly, efforts to bring about de-escalation involve either *control* or *resolution*.

INTERPERSONAL CONFLICT:
SUBSTANTIVE AND EMOTIONAL ISSUES

Concepts and Illustrative Diagnoses

A major distinction is drawn between substantive and emotional conflict. *Substantive issues* involve disagreements over policies and practices, competitive bids for the same resources, and differing conceptions of roles and role relationships. *Emotional issues* involve negative feelings between the parties (e.g., anger, distrust, scorn, resentment, fear, rejection). This distinction and many specific types of interpersonal issues are illustrated by our three case histories.

The cases contained several instances of "philosophical differences," which of course are usually manifested in conflicts over the substance of policies and practices. For example, Sy disapproved of the controller's relative orientation to headquarters versus the local management. Other examples are provided by the Charles–Fred case: the personnel manager disagreed with the way the superintendent handled absenteeism, disciplinary action, and union-management relations. In turn, the superintendent disagreed with the personnel manager's approach to the union president.

Some substantive issues centered on a type of "role invasion." Charles perceived Fred as usurping his role and initiative in personnel matters. Fred countercharged that Charles had a narrow jurisdictional view of organizational responsibilities. In another case Lloyd was demanding that Bill share with Lloyd's group more of the higher-level professional work and more of the control over design decisions. Bill clearly resisted changing what he saw as his primary responsibility for the authority over the total project.

Perhaps opposite to role invasion is "task deprivation," whereby one party is not getting the services which he requires in order to perform effectively. Sy and his manufacturing group were not satisfied with the service provided by the controller's office. Sy also claimed that he was not getting the assistance he needed from Mack on the new X-Mill project. In the Fred–Charles case, the former believed that Charles as personnel manager should have provided problem-solving assistance to manufacturing, rather than taking an aloof, blaming stance.

Another very frequently encountered source of interpersonal conflict in organizations is a "competitive incentive structure." It appeared in only one of the cases and even then our inference is speculative. Given Lloyd's reaction to the talk with his superior on the future structure of the OSP project, perhaps an unstated issue between Bill and Lloyd had been a mutually recognized competition for formal leadership of the OSP effort if and when it were approved for implementation.

Turning to emotional issues, one type is "personal need deprivation," wherein the situation is currently failing to satisfy some salient personal needs. For example, Mack was frustrated because the controller's job required attention to detail and a resource-conservation orientation which were not natural to him, and the job denied him opportunities to be expansive and to be a promoter which would be more gratifying for him. Also, Mack's failure to get the X-Mill project made him envious of Sy. In the Bill–Lloyd case, Lloyd experienced several types of need deprivation his competance was not sufficiently recognized, his uniqueness as an individual was not being confirmed, and he was not feeling included. Bill was in a position to allow Lloyd to better fulfill these needs without necessarily denying some of his own. Probably Bill's denial was largely inadvertent.

In the case of "incompatible personal needs," two persons make contradictory demands on their situation or on their relationship, demands which are based directly on their respective interpersonal needs. For example, in work sessions, Mack evinced a relatively high need to control and to be aggressive, which violated Sy's need to collaborate in a less highly charged atmosphere. Drawing upon the Bill-Lloyd conflict, we observed a contradiction between Bill's personal preference for fluid, permissive relationships, and Lloyd's preference for more structure, clarity and "crispness."

Even where it is not clear what personal needs are being blocked, "differences and similarities in personal styles" may be threatening to the persons involved. For example, Fred and Charles were each annoyed by the other's general personal style: Fred viewed Charles as academic, indirect, and cautious; Charles regarded Fred as impulsive and inconsiderate of others. Each perceived the other as lacking in humility and overly defensive. In fact, it appears that each was most annoyed by certain behaviors of the other which also typified their own pattern (e.g., lecturing and using cross-examination style in discussions).

Both substantive and emotional issues were involved in all three cases, although in differing degrees. In the Mack—Sy case the substantive issues paled in comparison with the personal issues. In the other two cases there was more balance between substantive and personal issues.

Implications

The distinction between substantive and emotional issues is important because the substantive conflict requires bargaining and problem solving between the principals and mediative interventions by the third party, whereas emotional conflict requires a restructuring of a person's perceptions and the working through of feelings between the principals, as well as conciliative interventions by the third party. The former processes are basically cognitive, the latter processes more affective.

TRIGGERING EVENTS:
PENETRATING BARRIERS TO ACTION

Concepts and Illustrative Diagnoses

According to our model, the interpersonal issues described above can and do exist as latent conflict for periods of time. The latent-manifest nature of interpersonal conflict is governed by the barriers to overt conflict actions and circumstances which nevertheless are capable of precipitating such actions.

A variety of barriers can prevent a party from initiating or reacting to either conflict or conflict-resolution actions. A party may be deterred from confronting an interpersonal conflict by internal forces such as attitudes, values, needs, desires, fears, anxieties, and habitual patterns of accommodating; and by external barriers, such as group norms against the expression of conflict, and physical obstacles to interaction. Examples of barriers include:

a) Task requirements (e.g., time limits inhibit direct confrontation of feelings and issues involved in a conflict).

b) Group norms (e.g., shared feelings that managers should not express negative feelings toward others).

c) Personal role concepts (e.g., a boss who feels his ability to engage in conflict with a subordinate is limited by his supervisory role).

d) Public images (e.g., desire to maintain an image of gentility).

e) Perception of the other's vulnerability (i.e., the other person may be seen as too susceptible to hurt from a direct expression of feelings).

f) Perception of one's own vulnerability to the other's conflict tactics.

g) Fear that a conciliatory overture won't be reciprocated.

h) Physical barriers to interaction.

Other specific examples drawn from the three cases will be identified below.

Despite actual or potential barriers such as the ones just named, some event or circumstance may be capable of precipitating a conflict cycle; it sets off a round of hostile interactions, a vigorous disagreement, a candid confrontation, or a problem-solving interchange. We refer to these stimuli as *triggering events*, and propose that they can have their effect either by increasing the magnitude or salience of the issues in the conflict or by lowering one of the barriers to action. If the issue is strictly substantive, the parties may engage each other when the substantive issue becomes relevant to an action or when other organizational circumstances require a decision. Or one may choose to explore the issue when the circumstances are especially favorable to the approach he will take, whether it be bargaining or problem solving. Not surprisingly, where emotional issues are involved, the ignition of manifest conflict is explicable in less rational terms; offhand remarks and criticism on sensitive points are typical triggering events.

Thus, diagnosis of an interpersonal conflict involves discovering what types of barriers are customarily operating and what triggers the conflict cycle. Below we diagnose these aspects of the three case studies.

In the Bill–Lloyd case, the barriers to direct mutual conflict were primarily internal to one party, namely Bill. He was inhibited and slightly intimidated by Lloyd's strong, aggressive, interpersonal style which Bill felt, limited *his* ability to engage in toe-to-toe exchanges in the larger group setting, and tended to make him procrastinate in confronting Lloyd outside the group. This assumption about Bill is supported by his comment that without the consultant's presence he probably would not have confronted Lloyd "at the process level" about Lloyd's domineering behavior.

The Lloyd–Bill conflict interchanges illustrate how conflict acts are easily triggered by a strong dose of the irritating condition, combined with a tempting tactical opportunity to put stress on the other conflict principal. The less inhibited Lloyd made Bill's life difficult in the joint staff meetings which contained many strong stimuli for Lloyd. The meetings exposed him directly to Bill's nonstructured style and reminded him that Bill's was the single leadership role differentiated within the group. In this setting Lloyd's only way of differentiating himself within the total group was through his own behavior. Besides, apparently Lloyd wanted to increase the stress on Bill in order to develop the latter's interest in reconsidering the *status quo*; the joint meetings afforded him an excellent opportunity to do just that.

The next question to address in this type of diagnosis of the Bill–Lloyd case is: what can occasion the mutual confrontation between participants who are managing so differently their respective sides of the conflict? Bill joined the conflict when he did because he felt mounting internal pressure and perceived new external support in the urgings of his superior and the availability of the consultant. During the confrontation meeting more specific circumstances precipitated Lloyd's openness about his emotional concerns–a development which proved important in creating a benevolent cycling of their interchanges. These circumstances included the growing evidence that Bill and Dave were listening to, accepting, and responding to the issues he had already identified.

The Mack–Sy case contains similarities, but also contrasts. Like Bill above, Sy was inhibited by the other person's (Mack's) typically aggressive pattern in meetings. Apparently, Sy tended to suppress his anger and withdraw from such situations rather than show his feelings toward Mack or pursue his side of a disagreement. Again like Bill, he was stimulated to join the issue when the consultant was present. In particular, the conflict interchange at cocktails was precipitated by the consultant's interviews, which led to a face-to-face meeting, which in turn was given focus by the consultant's suggestion that they work on their relationship. Sy's more spontaneous outburst at the staff meeting resulted from a combination of factors: he experienced mounting frustration at not having made headway on the dialogue; he perceived support from the presence of the consultant and other members of the staff; he had just witnessed a gross example of Mack's aggressiveness; and finally he had just suffered the criticism directed at an area of his responsibility.

It is significant that in this instance, despite his typically aggressive style, Mack's barriers prevented *him* from really joining the conflict issues in these two meetings during the consultant's first visit. One barrier was fear—he feared the conflict's potential adverse consequences for his future. Another barrier was limited emotional energy—he was already preoccupied with his current career dilemmas. The third barrier was tactical disadvantage—Sy had the initiative and Mack may have felt off balance.

The Fred—Charles case illustrates a comparatively simple pattern. There were no significant barriers except the typical organizational norms against manifest conflict. Charles' organizational insecurity might have operated to some extent to inhibit him in completely opening up on Fred. However, Charles' own conflict initiatives were in part precipitated by the presence of his boss who had been urging him to take more risks in his relations with other departments, a factor which clearly nullified the tendency to be inhibited because of his organizational insecurity. Apart from that indirect stimulus to conflict, either party was quick to engage the other whenever he was presented with an example of the other's behavior which he disliked. Therefore, unlike the other two pairs of principals, Fred and Charles engaged in shorter and more frequent cycles of mutual conflict.

Implications

The above type of case-by-case analysis of barriers and triggering events opens up some possibilities relevant to the constructive management of conflict.

First, an important aspect of conflict management is choosing the right issue, time and place for joining the conflict. An understanding of barriers and triggering events is essential in effectuating this choice. If one wants to prevent manifest conflict—at least temporarily—one can preserve and bolster the types of barriers which are effective in the case at hand, and take steps to head off the types of events which trigger a conflict interchange. Conversely, if the situation is otherwise appropriate for constructive dialogue and one wants to precipitate the conflict, he knows what types of barriers must be overcome and what types of factors are likely to make the conflict especially salient for each principal. Because a different set of barriers and precipitating factors usually applies to each principal, it is important to find that subset of circumstances which facilitates a mutual confrontation.

Second, for a particular interpersonal conflict, some events will trigger conflict tactics which initiate a malevolent cycle and others trigger conflict-resolution efforts which have higher potential for initiating a benevolent cycle. Diagnosing a particular conflict involves distinguishing between these two types of circumstances.

Third, an analysis of events which surround or precede a conflict interchange often provides clues regarding the basic issues in the recurrent conflict.

Fourth, the frequency of conflict encounters may be systematically controlled by operating on barriers and triggering events, a point discussed in a later section on the operational objectives of conflict management.

CONFLICT TACTICS, RESOLUTION
OVERTURES AND THEIR CONSEQUENCES

Concepts and Illustrative Diagnoses

Conflict tactics and resolution overtures manifest the conflict. They include expression of feelings of conflict (anger, attack, avoidance, rejection) and feelings of conciliation (regret, sympathy, warmth, support). They also include both the competitive strategies intended to win the conflict, such as blocking, interrupting, deprecating others, forming alliances, out-maneuvering the adversary, and one-upmanship; and the cooperative strategies intended to end the conflict, such as unilateral or reciprocal concession and search for integrative solutions.

The potential costs and benefits of interpersonal conflict include those that affect each of the participants personally (in psychological and career terms), their work, and others around them, including colleagues, superiors, and subordinates. These costs can accrue from merely knowing that one is in an antagonistic relationship, from the manifest tactics of the other and of oneself, and from the reactions of nonparticipants to the conflict. Included in the costs of conflict are the missed opportunities for creative collaboration as well as the more tangible current consequences. Below we review the three cases in terms of conflict-relevant acts and their consequences.

What if Bill and Lloyd had failed to ameliorate the situation or resolve the issues which divided these two directors? The case illustrates organizational consequences of tension in general and tactics of commission and omission in particular. The tension between them and between their respective groups had the potential effect of decreasing the productivity of the OSP effort and lowering the morale of the professionals involved, increasing turnover, etc. Several tactics had adverse effects on the project: Lloyd could have expected to mount increasing criticism about the status of the OSP. It would have probably become increasingly difficult for Bill to cope with Lloyd in the joint sessions. Bill's pattern of ignoring the potential contribution Lloyd could make also would have affected the quality of the joint effort. If continued, these conflict tactics would have helped perpetuate the conflict, whatever the original issues.

One tactic of Lloyd's—his proposal to reassign personnel—had even more potential for escalating the conflict. If Lloyd had fulfilled his threat and requested that some members of his professional staff be transferred permanently to Bill's group, he would have brought the unresolved conflict to the attention of their superiors. This development would have been embarrassing to one or both, and would have led to more intergroup maneuvering and more antagonism. At the same time such transfers did represent one solution to otherwise unresolved conflict—it would have reduced the intergroup interdependence and separated the main antagonists, Bill and Lloyd.

In addition to the adverse effects of the conflict on the organization described above, the case illustrates psychological costs for the participants: for Bill, personal disappointment if the total group's process reverted to an earlier pattern and harrassment from a tough adversary; for Lloyd, discomfort with Bill's style and exclusion from an opportunity to contribute and thereby experience enhanced self-worth.

The Bill-Lloyd case also illustrates certain plausible gains of conflict—for both the organization and the participants. Some level of rivalry and tension between the two directors and between the two groups of professionals might enhance motivation, ensure a productive level of criticism, and increase the available number of alternative solutions to technical problems. Apparently, this productive level of tension would persist even if the major conflict issues between Bill and Lloyd were resolved. Psychologically, there were also potential gains (e.g., Lloyd appeared to the consultant to rather enjoy aspects of the interpersonal conflict, as if he personally was energized by it).

In the Mack-Sy case, the psychological cost which resulted from their interpersonal conflict was a dominant consideration. Sy had singled out his relationship with Mack as the one about which he was "especially concerned." Similarly, Mack had referred to an "intense" conflict before he made it apparent that the other person was Sy. Mack was anxious about the risks to his career associated with Sy's antagonism.

The conflict between Sy and Mack had been surfaced only in the one staff meeting, when Sy and his subordinate had placed on the agenda the item "role of the controller." Prior to that the conflict had not come to the attention of other staff members. Therefore, although it had affected the work of Sy and Mack and thereby their respective areas, the conflict had not had apparent consequences of particular importance for other groups in the system.

Another potential cost of the conflict had not fully materialized. In this organization a manifest, visible conflict between two aspiring managers could be costly to their careers. One criterion for promotability generally recognized in the organization was that a manager be able to work effectively with others. This apparently was an especially important consideration for Sy, who felt he had to demonstrate interpersonal competence to his superiors and to himself.

In contrast with the other two cases, there was no basis for hypothesizing any gains to either party from the continuation of the interpersonal conflict.

The confrontations played a role in coordinating their efforts to resolve and/or control their conflict. After the conflict escalated to Sy's climactic outburst at the staff meeting, the conflict was de-escalated. An early indication of a trend toward resolution was Mack's initial self-disclosures in the reconciliation session, suggesting that he had developed confidence in Sy's integrity. Their expressions of mutual concern in the encounter during the consultant's second visit constituted a further step toward resolution. Evidence of partial resolution accompanied by constructive control of any residual negative feelings between the principals was provided by their effective working together in meetings observed by the consultant. While the two men were not close friends, they were able to manage any continuing conflict.

The Fred–Charles conflict manifested itself in the following conflict tactics:

a) Fighting or arguing in front of others.

b) Criticizing each other for their performance.

c) Blaming each other for problems.

d) Lecturing each other.

e) Questioning, challenging each other's judgment.

f) Attributing negative qualities to the other, positive qualities to self.

g) Charles "piled on" or showed pleasure when Dave would confront Fred with some aspect of his behavior about which Fred was not especially proud.

h) Whenever he could, Charles attempted to ally himself with the consultant or the chief engineer.

i) Charles used a cross-examination style of discussing issues with Fred.

There were certain direct adverse effects on performance. Initial differences of opinion were exaggerated and polarized; they became difficult to resolve without someone feeling defeated. The conflict made substantial demands on the energy of all participants in the staff and in the interdepartmental relations. And yet, issues like absenteeism which required joint effort were not being handled effectively. There was the risk that forthcoming labor negotiations might be handled badly by management.

The conflict had implications for Charles' career. He could not be embroiled in conflict with the manager of the major group his department serviced and still hope to improve the general manager's confidence in him. While his conflict with the superintendent was not the principal reason for his termination, and while the confrontation had provided encouragement that the conflict would be worked through, the fact is that this peer conflict may have been an issue between Charles and his boss.

What were the psychological costs and gains for the participants? Fred reported some embarrassment about losing his objectivity and sharing so much about his feelings toward Charles in a meeting involving several members of management. He evidenced some guilty feelings about "laying into" Charles in the presence of the latter's subordinates. Interestingly, the same confrontation included a fringe benefit for Charles. He was pleased at being able to demonstrate to the general manager a willingness to take some risks.

Fred's reactions to Charles' interpersonal style included "seething," "ground," "strained to the limit." He was easily "teed off" by what he regarded as Charles' distrust, was annoyed at the "excessive criticism" by Charles and the "patness" of Charles' answers, in particular the latter's tendency to place all of the blame on Fred.

Charles, in turn, felt personally crowded and his role usurped whenever Fred would "get the bit in his teeth and go charging off without worrying about the implications for others." He felt excluded from the relationship between the superintendent and union president.

These qualitative descriptions of the principals' reactions to each other do not indicate the magnitude of strain or stress which they experienced. The consultant involved in all three cases judged the stress here to be less than that involved in the Mack—Sy case but slightly more than that in the Bill—Lloyd case. Moreover, both principals seemed relatively able to tolerate conflict and characteristically to enjoy a moderate level of conflict. Nevertheless, for neither of them was this contest more exhilarating than debilitating.

Most of the conflict tactics employed in the Fred—Charles case had the effect of perpetuating the conflict—both in the limited sense of the immediate argument and in the longer sense of providing more fuel for future conflict. The fighting, criticizing and blaming interchanges were especially difficult to terminate because each wanted to have the last word. A few of the tactics seemed to have more potential for escalating the conflict; for example, challenges regarding the other's judgment escalated to include a derogatory tone used by both. Recall Fred's assertion that even a production manager like himself could see that the decision obviously would *not* have the labor-relations implications Charles was alluding to. In turn, Charles was depreciating in tone when he quoted his subordinate's remark about the superintendent's not having anything better to do than second-guess the personnel department on the price of milk. These remarks took the form of personal attacks that were designed to hurt.

What were the principals' conflict-resolution behaviors in the Fred—Charles case? They were fewer in number and frequency but included:

a) The very acts of mutually agreeing to meet.

b) Instances where they listened to each other.

c) Charles' expression of regret for having "piled on."

d) Fred's acknowledgment that Charles had made an authentic expression of regret.

e) Fred's nondefensive acknowledgment of the fact that he had just bypassed Charles on a personnel-department matter, when it was pointed out by the consultant.

Implications

An understanding of the various species of conflict tactics is relevant to conflict management because conflict behaviors are the most available indices of the existence of differences between persons, and because the nature of the tactics largely determines the consequences of the conflict. Perhaps the most important diagnostic aspect of conflict management is an understanding of the consequences of an interpersonal conflict. The relevance is threefold.

First, an appreciation of the magnitude of costs is essential. Do the costs of conflict outweigh the gains, are they significant, and do they justify the costs of mounting an effort to achieve a better management of the conflict?

Second, an analysis of the particular consequences of a recurrent conflict usually provides an understanding of why the conflict is tending to escalate, de-escalate, or maintain itself. The analysis can indicate the connections between the conflict or conflict-management tactics which are used and the tendency for issues to proliferate or decrease in number.

Third, an understanding of the consequences of the current conflict, combined with an appreciation of the issues involved, enables one to identify the outcomes which are desirable and realistic and to map general strategies for achieving the desired outcomes. Typically these involve strategies of de-escalation, whether through conflict control or conflict-resolution approaches.

PROLIFERATION TENDENCIES

Of the total number of issues identified with each of the interpersonal conflicts analyzed in this study, probably some fraction were more basic and developed earlier in the relationship. Diagnosing the conflicts requires determination of which issues are basic and which are merely symptomatic, representing a proliferation of the basic issues. Issue proliferation occurs for a variety of reasons.

Umbrellas: Issues that Legitimate the Conflict

A party may inject a second or substitute issue into the conflict because it provides a more legitimate umbrella for the conflict. Substantive issues are often injected into a basically emotional conflict for this reason. For example, Sy's act of placing the "role of the controller" on the agenda characterized the issue as primarily a substantive one and therefore a relatively acceptable basis for challenging Mack. Similarly, Lloyd led off with the substantive intergroup issues, which were more likely to be seen as a justifiable basis for their interpersonal conflict.

Some types of substantive issues are often not stated but underlie other stated issues which are more legitimate grounds for disagreeing with each other. An example of a frequently unstated issue is the competitive incentive for two individuals who are considered for the same promotional opportunities or other organizational rewards. As noted above, this may have entered into the Bill–Lloyd case; also, Mack's negative feelings resulted in part from losing a competition to Sy.

Facsimiles–For More Cautious but Relevant Work

Symptomatic issues are sometimes reflections of the basic issues–in either content or form. For example, the substantive-intergroup issues raised initially by Lloyd–an opportunity for his professionals to have more influence and a higher quality of contribution–were very similar to the emotional issues which he later identified as personal concerns; namely, his desire to be more included and recognized as a competent professional. Although we cannot be certain that in this case the intergroup issue was merely a surface issue, it helps illustrate the frequently encountered pattern that explains the use of issues which are facsimiles of the basic one. There are at least three tendencies involved. First, the basic issue sometimes risks so much embarrassment for one or both persons that they can save face by acting as if their differences centred on some other issue. Second, if this is so, it is more "expressive" and therefore more gratifying for a person to engage another around a surface issue which is, nevertheless, similar to (rather than different from) the underlying issue. Third, by identifying a surface issue which resembles the basic issue, one is better able to exchange ideas (one's own perceptions of other's views) which are also relevant to the basic issue.

Bundling Boards: Issues that Guarantee Separateness

Issues may be added to further differentiate a pair in emotional conflict. Substantive issues may develop subconsciously from emotional conflicts, as merely another way one person can differentiate himself from a person toward whom he feels antagonistic. The introduction of these issues, unlike the use of "umbrellas," is the result of a spontaneous desire to bicker, rather than of a cognitive, tactical attempt to legitimate the conflict. Such may have been the nature of the spontaneous debate between Charles and Fred in the staff meeting, in which the issue *per se* was demonstrated to be of no practical importance. The parties themselves may remain largely unaware that their substantive disagreement derives from their mutual desire to differentiate themselves from each other. The underlying factor may be more apparent to their associates than to themselves.

Seizing the High Ground–To Ensure Tactical Advantage

Added issues may be tactically initiated by one party in the interest of pursuing his side of the conflict: sometimes a new substantive issue is injected tactically into the conflict by a party who wishes to gain the offensive or counter an opponent's offensive. This was a familiar pattern in the Fred–Charles case. For example, during his initial phone conversation with the consultant, Fred was smarting from Charles' criticism of the way he had neglected the absenteeism problem. By identifying the fact that he was working short-handed as a result of the failures of Charles' department, he reflected this inclination to inject an issue allowing him an offensive position. Charles reflected a similar propensity to insert new issues to regain the offensive. When Fred was reiterating his earlier criticism of the personnel department's pricing of the milk dispensed in the plant, Charles raised a question about whether, as superintendent, Fred was neglecting higher-priority responsibilities by worrying himself about the price of milk. This phenomenon is a form of escalation, one which is likely to invite further escalation. For one thing, it is usually very apparent to the other party that the first has injected a new issue the purpose of which is to put him on the defensive and inflict damage. Moreover, the issue is usually selected for its ability to inflict high damage on the target with relatively little risk for the initiator. Sometimes two parties can quickly see where this will lead, and if they have both established their respective second-strike capabilities, they drop back to the central issue, each with a higher sense of the potential cost of failing to reach some accommodation.

The Provocative Potential of Self-Defense

Additional issues sometimes result from attempts to cope with the consequences of primary conflict. For example, what Sy regarded as Mack's primary orientation to Detriot may have been Mack's way of coping with the anxiety he felt about his status with Sy and the general manager. Thus, Mack's effort to take defensive measures to cope with the conflict became a new source of conflict as far as Sy was concerned. The result is an unexpected escalation or at least a perpetuation of the conflict cycle.

Implications

Let us generalize the above discussion, returning to the earlier distinction of substantive and emotional issues. On the one hand, emotional conflict tends to create substantive disagreements which help the parties differentiate and separate themselves. Also, two parties may cooperate in using substantive issues to legitimate engaging each other in conflict; or one may use a substantive issue to help him prevail over his emotional adversary.

On the other hand, substantive conflict may create emotional conflict, hostility, and lowered trust. Two basic mechanisms are involved. One is the need for consistency. If one dislikes the position another takes, or if he is in competition with him, there is a psychological tendency to develop similar attitudes toward the person. The second mechanism involves the tactics of competition, debate, and bargaining over substantive differences; such tactics contain many points of friction and are likely to result in feelings of being attacked, in perceptions that the other is unfair, etc.

This analysis helps explain why all three conflicts had an abundance of both substantive and emotional issues. The general tendency postulated here is the proliferation of issues. Whether the original and basic issue is substantive or emotional, the conflict is likely to develop additional issues symptomatic of both types. Thus, even though these three cases did not have long histories, by the time the parties confronted there existed a large number of points of conflict. These many issues were surfaced one-by-one; the principals and the third party continuously confronted choices of which issues to treat.

This tendency for one type of conflict to generate the other has several particular consequences. When emotional conflict seduces the parties into projecting some substantive disagreement, one or both parties may be embarrassed to discover they are vigorously advocating positions about which they are basically uncertain or indifferent; in fact, their current position may be inconsistent with other positions they have taken, a fact which will not escape their colleagues. Further, by locking in on substantive issues, they generate the possibilities for more tangible win-lose contests; this condition has its own perpetuation dynamics.

When substantive conflict gives rise to emotional conflict, the latter creates "noise" in the interpersonal-interaction system upon which the parties must rely for confronting the substantive issues. For example, if the most basic issues in the Fred—Charles conflict arose out of their differing conceptions of the staff-line relationship, the emergent patterns of distrust and ego-bruising interchanges virtually ensured that they could not work rationally and effectively on the more substantive staff-line issues.

If two persons confront initially on the symptomatic issues, they can sometimes decrease the costs of conflict, and even create a climate favorable for confrontation on the more basic issues. However, *both* parties must have an appreciation that the issues being dealt with are symptomatic and not basic. Otherwise, they are likely to have unrealistic expectations of harmony; and they are more likely to create new symptomatic issues inadvertently.

If the parties can individually or jointly gain an appreciation of how issues have been added on, they are better able to reconceive the present conflict in its more essential, original terms. It becomes more apparent that part of the total conflict which exists between them is a result of a few essential conflict issues.

One of the purposes of dialogue between persons in extensive (multiple-issue) conflict with each other is to allow the parties to identify the more basic issues. In particular, the climate of acceptance in a confrontation group influences whether a person will "own up to" his feelings—the nature of the emotions he has invested in the conflict.

IMPLICATION OF THE MODEL
FOR CONFLICT MANAGEMENT

We have now explored each of four basic elements of a conflict episode. We have also analyzed how and why interpersonal conflicts tend to proliferate issues and thereby undergo escalation. At the same time, the increased costs of conflict tend to heighten the participants' interest in somehow arriving at a better management of the conflict.

Included in the earlier treatment of each element and of the proliferation tendencies is some discussion of their implication for conflict management. The discussion of implications is continued here, with particular focus on the operational objectives of conflict management

Let us continue to assume that we are referring to conflicts that are judged to have more dysfunctional than functional consequences for the principals and/or others, and that there exists a desire to manage the conflict more constructively. Typically, the most general operational objective is to interrupt a self-maintaining or escalating-malevolent cycle in one way or another and to initiate a de-escalating-benevolent cycle. Conflict management usually involves this objective whether the ultimate goal has been defined as control (minimizing the costs of the conflict without changing the basic issues in dispute), or resolution (eliminating the negative feelings and disagreements).

Each of the four elements of a conflict cycle suggests an operational measure of escalation and de-escalation, and identifies a corresponding target of conflict management. Three involve control; one requires resolution.

Preventing Ignition of a Conflict Interchange

One possible operational objective of conflict management might be to reduce the frequency of conflictful encounters where they have proved destructive in the past.

To implement this control strategy one must clearly understand the factors which represent inhibitors or barriers to conflict actions on the part of each principal. These can be bolstered or at least not inadvertently lowered. One must also have some knowledge of the potential triggering events so that these can be avoided or blunted when they occur. It is especially helpful to recognize "early warning signals"—signs that one or both parties are experiencing mounting stress.

This can be illustrated by the Mack—Sy case. Certain aspects of the conflict between these persons could be controlled and/or avoided. If each found the other's style irritating (Sy complained that Mack was domineering; and Mack, that Sy was compulsive and detail-oriented), each could attempt to overlook the behaviors involved and minimize their face-to-face contact. This essentially is what Sy was attempting to do when he would terminate meetings with Mack after he had become too agitated to continue. Also, Sy promoted his contacts with Mack's subordinate rather than with Mack personally whenever that served the same purpose. Because in their situation there was a relatively steady turnover of personnel in the positions they currently held, it might have been feasible to attempt to merely "control" the conflict between these two men.

Generally, however, the drawback to control strategies which aviod conflict exchanges is that the eventual results may be less desirable than an early expression of the conflict:

a) the conflict may tend to go underground, become less direct but more destructive, and eventually become more difficult to confront and resolve;

b) the participants' supression of the issues and their inclination to act on their conflicting beliefs and feelings may result in an accumulation of feelings that will make the manifest conflict—when it does occur—more intensely violent, and perhaps destructive.

One difficulty with the particular control strategy of preventing ignition of manifest conflict, especially via support for the barriers to expression of the conflict, is that such barriers tend to prevent potentially constructive confrontations as well as other tactical exchanges. For example, a norm against expression of interpersonal antagonism does not differentiate between those conflicts where control is the more appropriate approach and where resolution is readily possible.

Obviously, taken by itself, it is a control strategy, pure and simple; it does nothing directly to resolve the issues in dispute. However, it can also be utilized as a part of a more complex strategy:

a) Sometimes it will help achieve a cooling off period which will allow for other resolution initiatives or control efforts.

b) It is an appropriate strategy for temporarily protecting the larger system from disruption.

c) As was pointed out in the earlier discussion of triggering events and barriers to conflict, they present an extremely important tactical possibility for achieving the best timing of confronting an issue.

Constraining the Form of the Conflict

The second operational objective does not try to prevent all conflict interchanges, but attempts to set limits on the tactics and weapons employed. Illustrations from other social settings are helpful here. One example could be the notion of a limited war and abstention from the use of chemical or nuclear weapons. Another example is provided by a frequent practice of boys' camps, namely, fights occur only with boxing gloves in the gym on Saturday afternoon. Conflicts in organizations are sometimes constrained by the following understanding: Substantive conflicts will be decided informally by a series of meetings between pairs in advance of the formal meeting in order to avoid the direct conflict of protagonists in the group. The assumption underlying such a constraint is that direct conflict in the group would take more energy, produce a lower-quality decision, and result in more interpersonal debris. If these expectations are based on past experience, constraints may represent the best conflict-management strategy currently available to this social system; however, the thrust of this project is that other alternatives should be considered.

Sometimes substantive conflicts must be pursued according to the group norm that, if one criticizes the recommendation of another person, he offers his own recommendation. The rule prescribes that if you attack, you must likewise expose yourself by "stating your alternative." Thus, a certain symmetry is achieved in the offensive-defensive stances of those who disagree.

Acts based on emotional conflicts are also sometimes the subject of certain proscriptions and prescriptions. A social system may attempt to inhibit interpersonal conflict acts that occur in the presence of bosses or subordinates, because they are assumed to increase the cost of the conflict without serving any constructive purpose. Norms may attempt to rule out the tactics of "interpersonal billiards" whereby one principal attacks the other through some third person. Similarly, the group may be sensitive about "ganging up" on an individual, and, therefore, outlaw two-on-one interpersonal-conflict situations. In some systems it develops that one of the few permissible forms of expressing interpersonal antagonism is via humor, because the tension-raising attack is accompanied by its own tension-release act and therefore usually does not result in mutual conflict engagements which are feared.

As a control strategy, constraining the form of the conflict can be used in various ways:

a) to protect a social system from the disruptive consequences of less restrained conflict;

b) to prevent a conflict from escalating by in fact ruling out those tactics which are most likely to be provocative;

c) to achieve some de-escalation by eliminating some tactics which were responsible for having added on some of the existing issues.

Coping Differently With the Consequences of Conflict

The third operational measure focuses directly on the costs of a given set of conflict acts: these can be minimized depending upon how the target person copes with them. One's coping techniques influence not only the current psychological costs he experiences, but also the extent to which he creates new issues or initiates a new cycle. Let us consider three coping techniques: First, ventilating one's feelings to a friend may not only release one's tension, but also serve as a substitute for direct or indirect retaliation that would add new issues to the conflict. Second, developing or activating additional sources of emotional support and reassurance (colleagues or family) may raise one's tolerance for the same level of manifest conflict with his primary principal. Third, generating alternatives that make one's future less dependent upon the person with whom one is in conflict is also a way of reducing the costs of conflict without necessarily altering its form or resolving the underlying issues.

Several of the above methods of coping with conflict are illustrated by the way Mack and Sy each managed his end of the conflict at different points. Mack coped with Sy's threat to his career by stating his fear and inviting reassurance which he received from Dave, albeit not from Sy. Mack's overtures to Sy during the period between the consultant's visits were not reciprocated—and Mack felt rejected. He coped with these feelings in part through expressing them in phone calls with Dave. Sy for his part was avoiding Mack in order to avoid the discomfort associated with dealing with him. Mack's adjustment to Sy involved suppressing some of his natural operating patterns in order to meet some of Sy's expectations. Also, Mack continued to consider leaving the firm—one way of coping, not merely with his conflict with Sy, but also with his failure to receive the assignments he wanted.

Notwithstanding the appropriateness of the control tactics described here and in the section on preventing ignition of conflict, the overall strategy of conflict management could not be based on control alone in the Mack—Sy case. Certain considerations suggested that attempts to avoid or control the conflict alone would not be successful: the many reinforcing, self-perpetuating aspects of their conflict pattern, with the further potential of actually escalating the conflict. For example, Mack's withholding assistance from Sy (which the latter resented), was undoubtedly related to the antagonism Sy communicated back to Mack.

Eliminating the Conflict Issues

The fourth operational objective of conflict management would be measured by the number and importance of the issues between the parties. The above strategies of control can have the effect of de-escalating the conflict to the extent of eliminating some of the symptomatic issues. However, eliminating the basic issues means resolving them—reaching agreement where disagreement persists, achieving trust where distrust prevails, etc. There is little to be said about this objective because it is the most obvious and straightforward, although it is often the most difficult to achieve.

6

CONFRONTATIONS AND STRATEGIC THIRD-PARTY FUNCTIONS

In this chapter we treat first the concept of interpersonal confrontation and then the potential strategic functions of third-party participation. The following ingredients in an interpersonal setting are postulated as strategic to productive confrontation:

1. mutual positive motivation,

2. balance in the situational power of the two principals,

3. synchronization of their confrontation efforts,

4. appropriate pacing of the differentiation and integration phases of a dialogue,

5. conditions favoring openness in dialogue,

6. reliable communicative signs,

7. optimum tension in the situation.

The discussion of each of these factors in the present chapter includes a proposition about the relevance of the factor to the success of a confrontation, a description of the underlying rationale or psychological mechanisms involved, and an analysis of those aspects of the three case studies which indicated tactical opportunities for third-party influence.

INTERPERSONAL CONFRONTATION

Differences between persons or groups in organizations can be handled permanently and exclusively by the strategies of avoidance, constraint, and improved coping methods, discussed in Chapter 5. A more direct approach to conflict management involves confrontation, hopefully leading to resolution, but failing that, to more constructive control strategies.

Confrontation refers to the process in which the parties directly engage each other and focus on the conflict between them. Interpersonal confrontation involves clarification and exploration of the issues in conflict, the nature and strength of the underlying needs or forces involved, and the types of current feelings generated by the conflict itself.

If well managed, the confrontation is a method: for achieving greater understanding of the nature of the basic issues and the strength of the principals' respective interests in these issues; for achieving common diagnostic understanding of the triggering events, tactics and consequences of their conflict and how they tend to proliferate symptomatic issues; for discovering or inventing control possibilities and/or possible resolutions.

There are several other secondary but extremely important consequences of the well-managed confrontation: when participants candidly express and accurately represent themselves to each other, they increase the authenticity of their mutual relationship and individually experience a sense of enhanced personal integrity. The very fact of having invested personal energy in a relationship usually increases their respective commitments to improve the relationship, provided there is at least some small basis for encouragement. Even when there is no emotional reconciliation, if the parties are able to explicitly or implicitly arrive at better coping techniques, they tend to feel more control over their interpersonal environment and less controlled by it. The idea that organizations are more effective if they "confront and problem-solve conflicts" in contrast with "smoothing" or "forcing" them is supported by persuasive reasoning,[1] plenty of anecdotal evidence,[2] and some systematic research.[3]

---

[1] Schmidt, W. and R. Tannenbaun, "Management of Differences," *Harv. Bus. Rev.* **38**, November-December 1960, pp. 107–115.

[2] Blake, R. R., H. A. Shepard and J. S. Mouton, *Intergroup Conflict in Organizations,* Ann Arbor: Foundation for Research on Human Behavior, 1964.

[3] Lawrence, P. R. and J. W. Lorsch, *Organization and Environment: Managing Differentiation and Integration.* Boston: Division of Research, Graduate School of Business Administration, Harvard University, 1967.

Interpersonal confrontations involve risks for participants because they require that a person be candid about his feelings as well as opinions. Openness about one's feelings in itself often violates organizational norms prescribing rationality and proscribing emotionality.[4] Moreover, additional risks are incurred by owning up to the personal needs, concerns, and doubts, as well as antagonistic feelings often integrally involved in an organizational conflict. For example, if one does'nt resolve the relationship issue, one's statements may serve to add further cause for the other's antagonisms. Moreover, one may feel even more vulnerable because of what the other knows about him. Thus, the task of conflict management includes maximizing the productivity of a confrontation and minimizing the risks involved.

Ensuring Mutual Motivation

Unless both parties have incentives for resolving or controlling the interpersonal conflict, the prospects for a confrontation are poor. Without adequate incentive on both sides, there will not be give-and-take, in the sense either of emotional interchange or substantive bargaining and problem solving. If one attempts to engage another to resolve a conflict and discovers that the latter has more to gain by continuing the conflict, he may experience net losses from the venture. Or, if the initiating party discovers that the second was not aware of the conflict or was aware but indifferent, this can sometimes result in embarrassment and frustration. If the preliminary task for the initiating party turns out to be one of generating some incentive for the second to respond, the situation should be so defined as early as possible. In any event, the third party's role will only become maximally relevant if and when mutual incentive develops.

Where he has an opportunity, the third party can make an explicit effort to learn each party's motivation to resolve or better control the conflict, as well as the time frame within which each party views the adverse consequences of the conflict, prior to a confrontation initiative on either party's part.

If the third party learns of some important dissimilarities in motivation not otherwise apparent to the parties, such information can influence the choice of delaying or avoiding a confrontation. Knowledge about asymmetry in motivation may also influence the level of energy the

---

[4]Argyris, C. *Interpersonal Competence and Organizational Effectiveness.* Homewood, Ill.: Irwin Dorsey, 1962.

more highly motivated party decides to invest, the way he paces himself, and his expectations about outcomes.

Let us review the motivational forces in our three case studies.

1. In the Bill–Lloyd case, Lloyd was the prime mover on renegotiating the terms of the intergroup relationship, but Bill had a compelling need to clarify and improve their interpersonal relationship. Lloyd's stated objections had established a bargaining point from which he could accede to more accommodating behavior if he were more satisfied with other terms of the relationship. Thus the important condition had developed that each was being inconvenienced by the other and both were aware of this interdependance. In this case, the third party played no role in either establishing or certifying the mutual incentive to resolve their conflict. Bill had informed Lloyd of his intentions; the fact that Lloyd had readily accepted Bill's invitation to a meeting to work on their differences indicated Lloyd had reciprocal interest.

2. Again, in the Fred–Charles case, both parties were troubled by the psychic costs of the conflict and the way their relationship interfered with their work. The consultant had this knowledge in advance of the confrontation meeting. Both parties had independently sought the involvement of the consultant. Moreover, in addition to their own personal motives to confront, they received encouragement from other members of the staff to work on their relationship. Finally, the general manager pressured them to get together on the disagreement surfaced during the staff meeting. The above conditions—in motivational terms—were all quite favorable for a confrontation. Only Charles' greater organizational insecurity made him somewhat more cautious in the confrontation.

3. The Mack–Sy case contained the most unfavorable motivational conditions initially, something not appreciated by the consultant prior to the confrontation. On the one hand, Sy's dependance on Mack was both short-run and intermediate run. He needed Mack's technical help and wanted to be able to demonstrate to his superiors (as well as to himself) that he was interpersonally competent and thereby qualified for promotion. On the other hand, Mack's dependence on Sy was primarily long-term and conditional on Sy's promotion. Therefore, if Mack helped Sy look good, he improved Sy's chances of being promoted and becoming

his boss. If he didn't help Sy and Sy was still promoted, he could never work for Sy. In fact, Sy would be able to stop his career in the company. These considerations increased Mack's incentive to both try to maintain contacts with top-level people in Detroit and begin to look for another job outside of the company. Mack was not without some current motivation to resolve the conflict; recall his statement to Dave that he would have to confront a particular person whom he didn't name at the time. He did, however, have relatively less immediate motivation. The principals and Dave only became fully aware of the asymmetry during the confrontation when the consultant asked Mack whether he felt dependent upon Sy, and the answer was "no." However, Mack's incentives for more resolution were heightened by the conflict once it had been surfaced—he began to fear that continued conflict with Sy might be a major liability to his own career, whether or not Sy became his boss.

Achieving Balance in Situational Power

Power parity in a confrontation situation is most conducive to success. Perceptions of power inequality undermine trust, inhibit dialogue, and decrease the likelihood of a constructive outcome from an attempted confrontation. Inequality tends to undermine trust on both ends of the imbalanced relationship, directly affecting both the person with the perceived power inferiority and the one with perceived superiority. Experimental studies indicate, however, that the psychological mechanisms operating in the two parties are different.

How does it look from the point of view of the lesser power? Perhaps the most basic reason why another's power advantages undermine one's trust toward him is a general appreciation of the tendency for power to be used by those who possess it.[5] Studies by Mulder[6] provide further support for and insight into the proposition that the greater the unfavorable power differential, the less affirmative the attitude of the weaker person toward

[5]Solomon, L. "The Influence of Some types of Power Relationships and Game Strategies Upon the Development of Interpersonal Trust," *J. Abn. Soc. Psych,* 61 2, 1960. Zander, A., A. R. Cohen, and E. Stotland. *Role Relations in the Mental Health Professions.* Ann Arbor: University of Michigan, Institute for Social Research, 1957.
[6]Mulder, M., R. van Dijk, T. Stelwagen, J. Verhagen, S. Soutendijk and J. Zwezerijnen, "Illegitimacy of Power and Positivity of Attitudes Toward the Power Person," *Hum. Rel.* November 1965.

the more powerful one. In this study three conditions of asymmetrical reward-and-punishment power were manipulated, and the low-power party's attitudes measured. The attitudes included both liking toward the high-power party and tendency to perceive similarities between himself and that party. The finding: the greater the power differential, the more negative the attitudes.

Why does a perceived power advantage undermine the stronger party's trust toward the weaker? A high-power party tends to underestimate the low-power party's positive intent. The existence of a power advantage may make a person more likely to interpret cooperative behavior by the other as compliant, rather than volitional. The result is that the other's cooperative behavior has less positive effect on the first party's liking and estimate of intent. This tendency derives from the peculiarities of causal attribution. Having high power increases one's tendency to assign a locus of cause to himself. Without a power superiority, he can assign the locus of cause internally to the other. An experiment by Thibaut and Riecken[7] studied subject's reactions to their own successful influence attempts. Under one condition, the influence target was a person perceived to have higher power and status than the subjects. Under the other condition he was perceived to have lower power and status. The results were consistent with the proposition stated above: subjects who received cooperative responses from a low-power person showed less increase in their liking for him than those who received cooperative responses from those of high power. Interpolating these experimental results, we assume that cooperation from an equal will produce more positive liking than will cooperation by a person who has power inferiority.

Power imbalances not only undermine trust; they can inhibit both the weaker and, to a lesser extent, the stronger party, with the effect that they do not advance their respective views in a clear and forceful manner. The stronger party often tends to feel, "Why should I have to elaborate my views?" Conversely, the weaker party can rationalize, "What's the use?" The consequence of this reticence is apparent when one further considers that a person usually is ready to modify his views on an issue only after he is satisfied he has presented and supported his own unique views.

Situational power in the confrontation can be affected by various factors. Mutual dependence, discussed in the preceding section, is one

---

[7] Thibaut, J.W. and H. W. Riecken, "Authoritarianism, Status, and the Communications of Aggression," *Hum. Rel.* 1955. 8, 95–120.

factor which tends to ensure that both parties will feel they have power in the situation. The more symmetrical the perceived interdependence, the more equality of power. Other variables that can contribute to perceptions of advantage or disadvantage in a confrontation situation include organizational status, power and security, personal skills in conflict encounters, and the presence or absence of allies.

Therefore, the third party can attempt to avoid an overall imbalance e.g., by offsetting skill disadvantages via certain ground rules, by active interventions which ensure equal air time to less assertive participants, by helping a person who feels "one down" to make his point, by including others who will provide relatively more support to the participant with less organizational power, etc. Let us review our case studies in terms of the situational power of the participants.

1. Regarding the Bill–Lloyd case, we have already confirmed that they both had adequate incentives to work on their conflict. Moreover, their situational power was in overall balance, with differentials in conflict skill and perceived sources of support offsetting each other. To elaborate, Lloyd's aggressiveness, his somewhat greater taste for conflict, and his relatively greater ability to directly stress the other person in encounters were offset by the fact that Bill derived relatively more reassurance than Lloyd from the presence of the third party.

2. Of the situational factors affecting perceived power in the Mack–Sy case, some favored Mack, some favored Sy. Our analysis of motivation to resolve the conflict indicated Sy had an asymmetrically higher immediate motivation, a factor subtracting from his sense of potency and increasing his frustration. However, Sy had the initiative during their first meeting. There are several other specific reasons why Mack might have felt "one down" in his encounter with Sy. First, Sy was the number-two man on the staff, and the director relied upon him as his sounding board. Second, Sy and his subordinate (who were also friends) had joined together to confront Mack in a recent staff meeting. Third, Dave had a longer-term consulting contact with Sy than with Mack. Fourth, the personnel manager did not have strong rapport with either Mack or Sy, but had had more contact with Sy. He was so new that he had not had the opportunity to indicate any attitude or abilities that could be of help to Mack in a confrontation like this. Moreover, the other staff member present in the Thursday staff meeting was also too new to appear to Mack to be a positive factor in the situation. Given this analysis, it was fortunate that Sy's subordinate was not also present for this Thursday confrontation.

When they met during the consultant's second visit, they met without any other staff members present. Recent phone conversations and face-to-face interchanges between Mack and Dave contributed to the development of a close relationship between them. Thus, there was an improvement in the balance of situational power for this meeting in which reconciliation occurred.

3. The Fred–Charles case contained symmetries on each of several dimensions relevant to situational power. Their respective motivations to resolve the conflict were of comparable magnitude. Both were skilled in engaging and holding their own in conflictful interchanges (albeit not necessarily in the techniques of conflict resolution). The third party was probably perceived as equally distant or close to both. Only the chief engineer was present for part of their confrontation; and he was chosen for his balanced positive relations with the two principals. Charles' relative organizational insecurity was one enduring unbalancing factor. On the other hand, Charles made several unsuccessful ploys designed to draw in the third party as an ally.

SYNCHRONIZING CONFRONTATION EFFORTS

If initiatives and readiness to confront are not synchronized, the conflict can become more difficult to resolve. In practice, two persons who would like to reach a better understanding of their apparent differences frequently do experience difficulty synchronizing their efforts to confront each other. One may choose a time and place not suitable to the other, who then tries to avoid the open confrontation. This avoidance is taken as a further rejection or an indication that the other prefers to play out the conflict by indirect means, etc. If the second party later tries to confront in a different situation, the first, in the meantime, may have resolved to handle the differences by avoidance or indirect means, and the second party is now offended, further aggrieved, and more resistant to an open confrontation. Thus, the initiatives to confront by one principal must be synchonized with the other's readiness for the dialogue, in order to avoid an abortive confrontation.

Similarly, positive overtures are likely to contribute more to conflict resolution when they are synchronized with the other's readiness to correctly interpret the overtures and reciprocate them. Positive overtures which are not reciprocated often increase the initiator's level of frustration and discouragement; he feels betrayed and, subsequently, it becomes harder for him to hear a positive overture from the other or to make one himself.

At least two kinds of psychological tendencies underlie the dynamics described here. The first is reciprocation: a person tends to reject someone who has appeared to reject him. The second is reinforcement: a person's tendency to make overtures decreases if his efforts do not receive positive responses. A third basic factor is involved: one's acts can usually be given more than one interpretation. A confrontation effort motivated by a sincere interest to clarify the issues so that they can be resolved may be seen simply as an attack; or a conciliatory move can be interpreted as a sign of weakness, rather than as a positive overture from a position of strength.

A review of the three cases will enable us to appreciate the importance of synchronization in practice, and to analyze the opportunities for third parties to be of assistance.

1. In the Bill–Lloyd case, both parties were prepared for the confrontation when it occurred, Bill having communicated to Lloyd his reason for asking to meet. The third party's very presence and limited availability helped synchronize their time perspectives for the confrontation.

2. Similarly, in the Fred–Charles case, the consultant synchronized at various levels. The staff-meeting discussion of how he should use his time allowed the parties to express in subtle ways any reluctance about confronting which either of them might have felt. This case, of the three studied here, contained decision-making processes which were most open to influence and required the greatest sharing of the initiative between the two principals. The third party also synchronized moves during the confrontation. For example, he discouraged Charles from expressing high optimism about the prospects of an early resolution (a kind of positive overture from him) when Fred would quickly counter with a pessimistic prediction (which Charles then experienced as a rejection.)

3. The Mack–Sy case provides an example of inadequate synchronization which we shall review in detail. Sy's relatively higher readiness was signalled by several early clues which the third party should have attended to. The interpersonal conflict had been first surfaced by Sy when he placed "the role of the controller" on the agenda. Also, Sy had named Mack in his preliminary interview with Dave, whereas Mack referred only to a conflict of some urgency. Following this pattern, it was Sy who invited Mack to the cocktail session and who initiated the confrontation both at cocktails and at the staff meeting.

Mack was less ready. His dependence on Sy was not as immediate as vice versa, he may have perceived a power disadvantage in the confrontation setting, and he may have felt some guilt and vulnerability for having withdrawn his assistance from the X-Mill project.

Despite the asymmetry in readiness, the principals did meet. The overall decision to meet and work on the Mack—Sy conflict was an outcome of a series of choices in which the third party played a significant role. Let us review those choice points.

First, Dave counseled Mack that there was an optimum time lag after a person returns from a sensitivity-training experience and undertakes heavy interpersonal work in an organizational context. If Mack accepted the notion, he would have been encouraged not to postpone his confrontation with Sy too long. In this early interview with Mack, however, Dave did not check whether the idea made sense to Mack, nor did he determine whom Mack felt he "had to confront." Dave didn't gain this information because of time limitations and because he didn't want to press Mack to identify his antagonist. Dave's stance was not particularly inappropriate at that time because he hadn't yet met with Sy nor entertained the idea of a confrontation. However, in view of later developments, it would have been valuable if Dave had taken special note of Mack's failure to name the other person involved, asking himself and perhaps Mack: Did the omission reflect a lack in Mack's trust or confidence regarding Dave or uncertainty in his perceptions of the consultant's role? Confronting Mack with this question would have been potentially embarrassing; however, in view of the fact that Dave and Mack were discussing Mack's recent experiences in which interpersonal openness was normal, the risks were probably minimal.

Second, Dave chose to mention to Sy the possibility of a meeting of the three of them during his current visit. Sy immediately bought the idea and provided the initiative for following through. Dave was ambivalent, and asked himself several questions before agreeing to the meeting. For example, he asked "Is Mack ready?" In fact, Mack had *not* indicated that he was ready for a confrontation with Sy. Dave relied upon inferences: Mack was currently wrestling with interpersonal issues; Mack had said he was determined to confront one member of the staff, whom Dave now assumed to be Sy. (And later this was confirmed.) The second question was more critical to Dave's decision to proceed: "Are Sy and Mack going to confront anyway?" Dave heard them both express resolve to confront the other. Dave believed the prospects of a constructive outcome were higher with a third party like himself present. He also quickly decided that he could assume his personal responsibility for the meeting and the risks entailed; and that he had the energy to work that evening.

Third, Dave did not question or delay Sy's act to invite Mack, although he felt uneasy about it at the time. Sy's action had the advantage of being spontaneous, directly expressing his interest in getting together, and increasing his commitment. A disadvantage of Sy's quick move was that he and Dave didn't have an opportunity to discuss what should be communicated to Mack about their expectations so that Mack's decision to join them would take these expectations into account. In inviting Mack to meet with himself and Dave, Sy apparently went no further than asking him to join them for drinks after work. Dave was uncomfortable in leaving it at this, but was more uncomfortable with the awkwardness of any existing alternative for contacting Mack before they met at the club. As a result neither Dave nor Sy ensured that Mack was aware of the agenda for the session. This denied him information which might have influenced his decision to accept the invitation and provided him with an opportunity to prepare himself mentally and emotionally. Dave only fully appreciated the degree of importance of this omission later in reviewing the entire episode.

Fourth, after they had been together for a brief period, the consultant indicated that his plans included the possibility of exploring and working on interpersonal relationships. Ordinarily, such a suggestion made to a group is not very coercive. It could be addressed or ignored. But in this case, three out of four already had this activity in mind. Clearly, Mack had less choice than Sy as to whether a confrontation would take place.

Dave's alternative at the outset of the meeting was first to share with Mack what had occurred in the afternoon and how it had been decided to meet; and then to allow Mack to react to the general idea of working on his relationship with Sy as well as to indicate whether this was the time and place.

To summarize the above discussion, the many decisions involved in arranging the first meeting and defining its purpose both reflected and contributed to the asymmetrical pattern of Sy's high readiness and Mack's low readiness for the confrontation. Ideally, the decision process would have had just the opposite effect—decreasing the asymmetry.

This asymmetry during Dave's first visit undoubtedly limited the progress which could be made in the meetings and may have enhanced Mack's sense of the risks involved and his feelings that the confrontation had been rigged. For Sy's part, the resulting lack of engagement by Mack served to increase his frustration.

In the period between Dave's visits, the asymmetry was reversed. Sy became *less* available than Mack for further work on their relationship. Sy was busy during this period, but other factors were probably involved. Apparently, Sy's confidence in his own ability to confront Mack in a one-to-one setting and talk through differences was lower than Dave had assumed. A comment Sy made at the end of Dave's first visit reflected this idea, but it did not fully register with Dave until he was reviewing the entire episode. In any event, when Sy declined to respond to Mack's bids to engage in dialogue, the latter felt rejected and discouraged.

Finally, in preparation for the reconciliation meeting during his second visit, the consultant not only ascertained that both principals were motivated to work on their relationship, but also ensured that the timing was right before he proposed the meeting to either one. The likelihood of a productive meeting was enhanced accordingly. During that meeting, the third party also intervened at the level of dialogue to ensure that Sy responded verbally to Mack after the latter had made a self-disclosure and had begun to feel anxious about the meaning of Sy's silence.

PACING THE DIFFERENTIATION AND INTEGRATION PHASES OF THE DIALOGUE

At least two phases of an effective conflict dialogue can be identified—a differentiation phase and an integration phase. The basic idea of the *differentiation phase* is that it usually takes some extended period of time for parties in conflict to describe the issues that divide them, and to ventilate their feelings about each other. This differentiation phase requires not only that a person be allowed to state his views, but also that he be given some indication his views are understood by the other principal.

An effective confrontation will involve an *integration phase* where the parties appreciate their similarities, acknowledge their common goals, own up to positive aspects of their ambivalences, express warmth and respect, and/or engage in other positive actions to manage their conflict.

A conflict-resolution episode does not necessarily include just one differentiation and one integration phase. It may be comprised of a series of these two phases; but the potential for integration at any point in time is no greater than the adequacy of the differentiation already achieved. Dialogues are likely to abort or to result in solutions that are to be unstable, to the extent that the parties try to cut short the differentiation phase. In our opinion, the principle referred to here has been dramatically illustrated in race relations where the antagonism between the races will require that blacks further differentiate themselves from whites (politically, culturally, physically) and establish respect for their differences before major integrative work will be viable. We have observed similar patterns in interpersonal relationships.

Incidentally, one requirement this imposes on the third party is that he be comfortable with both (a) a high level of sustained differentiation and the hostility and assertions of opposing goals that characterize the differentiation phase; and (b) the warmth and closeness often expressed as a part of the integration phase.

These two phases can be identified in all three cases. One case (Bill—Lloyd) illustrates the use of a third party for only one phase. The session in which Dave participated accomplished the differentiation. The only really integrative acts were to express confidence in their ability to continue the dialogue in general and to agree to a joint meeting of their groups in particular. The substance of the integrative phase was continued later.

The Mack—Sy case illustrates a differentiation phase involving two intensive sessions and one low-key session in which the conflict atmosphere had de-escalated (but no substantive or real emotional *interpersonal* work had been accomplished between Mack and Sy. The interpersonally integrative session occurred many weeks later.

The Fred—Charles case perhaps best illustrates our view of these phases and also suggests some of the aspects of the dialogue format which correlate with these phases and can be influenced by the third party. The first phase of the Fred—Charles conflict occurred at the office and was confined to three persons. It involved clarification of divisive issues, identification of personal differences, a there-and-then orientation (reviewing past events), and escalation of ego-bruising behaviors. The second phase—at the restaurant and in an enlarged group—involved emphasis on common goals, identification of personal similarities between the principals, and a here-and-now orientation.

Stated in more general terms, the components of this sequence in the Fred—Charles case were:

a) divisive, differentiating agenda followed by integrating topics;

b) task issues followed by personal reactions;

c) there-and-then discussions giving way to more attention to the here-and-now process;

d) simple social groupings gradually complicated by adding other persons (the preconfrontation phone interviews were followed by the three-person group which was then enlarged to include another person);

e) work setting followed by more informal setting.

PROMOTING NORMS, ADDING REASSURANCE, AND EMPLOYING SKILLS THAT FAVOR OPENNESS

Interpersonal confrontations frequently founder because the principals do not feel that they can be open with each other about their private opinions, perceptions, and feelings, which comprise the essential data for understanding their current conflict and finding a way to work out of it Three factors significantly contribute to openness in the dialogue of a particular confrontation: relevant norms of the social system, the emotional reassurance available to the participants, and the "process skills" available for facilitating dialogue.

Normative Support for Openness

In all three cases there were many factors supporting openness in interpersonal relationships. All six principals previously had participated in a sensitivity-training workshop which emphasized the value of openness about feelings and confrontation of interpersonal differences. In the Bill—Lloyd case, these norms had become a part of the working process of the larger OSP group. Lloyd was aware that Bill and George (Lloyd's predecessor in the liaison role) had an open relationship. In both the Mack—Sy and Fred—Charles situations, their superiors and colleagues had also participated in this type of training experience and typically expressed support for the values of openness; nevertheless, these managers experienced considerable difficulty in applying the recommended techniques of openness and confrontation to their organizational relationships. In all three cases, undoubtedly the presence of a third-party consultant associated with sensitivity training further strengthened the normative support for openness, and helped structure the setting for dialogue. Where the potential participants of a confrontation previously have not had an experience comparable to sensitivity training, separate sessions between the third party and the principals can provide the latter with the individual practice and training in confronting, openness, expression of feelings, feedback, process analysis, etc.

Reassurance and Acceptance Available

One of the reasons for not confronting an issue is that exposing an underlying issue in a conflict means owning up to resentments, rejections, and other feelings that the person himself doesn't like to admit. Many of us have been brought up to regard these feelings as "petty" and "silly" and as "being too sensitive." Also, as was stated in Chapter 5, one may believe that these feelings result from insecurities (about his competence or his acceptance) that he is unwilling to acknowledge, either to himself or to someone else.

The presence of a third-party consultant, whose role is assumed to require noncritical detachment and who can provide acceptance and emotional support, is reassuring to the participant to a confrontation. He can assume that there is a greater likelihood that someone present will accept his feelings without evaluating them.

Process Skills Available.

In all three cases, the third-party consultant was perceived by the parties as decreasing the risk of an abortive confrontation. By being identified as a "sensitivity trainer," he was assumed to possess substantial skills at facilitating such processes; therefore the parties perceived less risk that the confrontation would bog down, become repetitive, and result in more frustration and perhaps bitterness. The third party may have slightly increased the potential payoff from these confrontations in the sense that participants believed that he could assist them in learning something of general value about their behavior in such situations. (Chapter 7 explores actual techniques which constitute process skill. Here we are interested in the reassurance for the participants, if they can assume that such skills are available.)

ENHANCING THE RELIABILITY OF
COMMUNICATIVE SIGNS

The confrontation will make no headway unless the principals each can understand what the other is saying. Even under conditions where the message sender is striving to be open about his intentions, opinions, feelings, and reactions to the other, various factors can limit the reliability with which the messages encoded by himself are decoded by the receiver.

A person responds to only some fraction of the information sent to him. Persons utilize and interpret the available information in ways which tend to confirm, rather than disconfirm, their existing views.[8] Two processes can contribute to this bias: selective perception and predisposed evaluation. Selective perception is the idea that a person perceives and utilizes information about which he has little ambivalence, avoiding information that challenges attitudes which are not firmly held.[9] Predisposed evaluation refers to the tendency to evaluate negatively, to discount, to refute information which one cannot avoid and which disagrees with one's existing attitudes.[10]

If a party is assumed to have done or said something he did not actually do, or if a party is perceived as pursuing objectives he is not in fact seeking, a third party can perform a communication function increasing the validity of mutual perceptions. By skillful intervention, a person may better understand his own position, especially his own doubts; and he may better understand the other's position, especially the limited character of the other's demands and the integrity of the other's motive.

There are several benefits to having accurate perceptions replace misperceptions which prompted or which fed a conflict. The person who achieves a more accurate perception can adjust to the reality. In addition, there is a possible psychological effect for the person who becomes better understood. When one finds that, despite efforts to explain himself, he is not understood, he tends to feel frustrated with the situation, angry toward those who do not understand him, and defensive about his views. These feelings contribute to the conflict. If and when he finally discovers he is more correctly perceived, he becomes more relaxed; he feels somewhat more accepted just by virtue of being understood; he is more likely to critically review his own position and to modify it in ways which are responsive to the other person's views.

A third party can contribute to the general reliability of the communicative acts by translating and articulating for the parties, by procedural devices, by developing a common language for the dialogue. In addition, as we have already explored, synchronization contributes to the accuracy of the interpretation of signs.

[8]Blake, R., and J. S. Mouton, "Comprehension of Own and Outgroup Positions Under Intergroup Competition," *J. Confl. Res.*, 1961, 5.
[9]Festinger, L., *A Theory of Cognitive Dissonance*, New York: Harper and Row, Publishers, Incorporated, 1957.
[10]Luchins, A. S., "Influence of Experience on Reactions to Subsequent Conflicting Information," *J. Soc. Psych.*, 1960, 51, pp. 367–385.

In each of the three cases, Dave frequently would summarize what he had heard one person say, and then check to see whether the person was satisfied with that statement. This appeared to have had several effects in the dialogues studied here. First, it demonstrated and reassured each person that he had adequately stated his position; or it provided an opportunity for him to make any corrections which he felt necessary. Second, when the consultant was restating one person's views, the other person had another opportunity to listen for and understand the first's concerns and preferences. Understanding is promoted by the fact that the person is less likely to distort messages from a neutral than from an adversary, and by any special ability which the consultant exercises in crystallizing the adversary's views. Third, in restating a person's views, the consultant endeavored to characterize a party's position in a way which made it understandable and justifiable. This can have the effect of reducing any guilt a person may feel associated with his own views and increase the other person's understanding and perhaps acceptance of the view.

As a procedure occasionally applied to the two participants, Dave would ask a person to repeat what he had just heard the other person say before he allowed the former to respond. A related procedure which is sometimes used with great success, but was not employed in these three cases, is "role reversal," where each person is asked to take the role of the other, to articulate and defend the other's position. Thus, the same dialogue between the principals is continued for a period of time with each playing the role of the other. Still another device sometimes used for similar purposes is a tape recording of the dialogue which can be replayed by the participants in order to achieve greater understanding of what each was trying to say.

In each of our three case studies, both principals understood the technical terms which were being used, and they shared important dialogue terminology, which they had learned in the sensitivity-training workshops they had attended. Therefore, Dave had only to add to and help refine the dialogue vocabulary. For example, principals used and understood the meaning of "feedback," the distinction between one's "feelings" and one's "thoughts," and between "basic issues" and "symptomatic issues." Beyond that, the pairs of principals needed to develop a language for signaling priorities (i.e., the relative importance each person attached to the grievances he had with the other); and for making important distinctions (e.g., to differentiate between the other's acts which challenge one's self-concept versus those acts which make one's task work more difficult). It is not clear just how much language development actually occurred in the cases, or whether the third party played an instrumental role in this development.

MAINTAINING A PRODUCTIVE LEVEL OF TENSION

The third party can influence the level of stress in the interpersonal system, which in turn affects the productivity of the dialogue. There is persuasive experimental evidence to support the theory of Schroder, Driver, and Streufert[11] which postulates that an individual's capacity for complex thinking is altered in a curvilinear fashion as stress increases; and that therefore, the individual's maximum ability to integrate and to utilize information occur at some *moderate stress level*. The more specific effects of very high stress include consideration of fewer alternatives, rigidity, and repetition;[12] reduction in the dimensionality of thinking (i.e., resulting in simpler perceptual systems), and reduction in the number of goals salient for the individual.[13] High stress also increases tendencies to perceive threat and use power.

Observations of third-party consultation supports the relevance of the curvilinear model to interpersonal conflict, just as the concept is incorporated in some theories of psychotherapy.[14] (See Fig. 6-1.) The idea that there is an optimum level of tension for an interpersonal confrontation can be understood by considering the probable results of three different levels of stress:

a) If the threat level is low, there is no sense of urgency, no necessity to look for alternative ways of behaving, and no incentive for conciliatory overtures.

[11] Schroder, H. M., M. J. Driver, and S. Streufert, *Information Processing Systems in Individuals and Groups.* New York: Holt, Rinehart and Winston, 1966.

[12] Osgood, C. E., *An Alternative to War or Surrender.* Urbana: University of Illinois Press, 1962.

[13] Milburn, T. W., "The Concept of Deterrence: Some Logical and Psychological Considerations," *J. Soc. Iss.* 1961, 17, pp. 3-11.

[14] Rogers, C. R. "A Theory of Therapy, Personality, and Interpersonal Relationships, as Developed in the Client-Centered Framework," in Sigmund Koch (Ed.), *Psychology: A Study of a Science.* Volume 3, pp. 184-256. New York: Mcgraw-Hill, 1959.

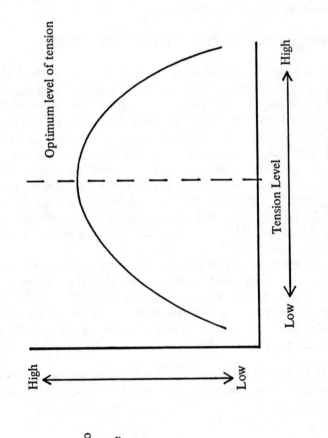

Figure 6–1. Relationship of Tension to Productivity in an Interpersonal Confrontation

b) At a higher threat level, say moderate level, the person searches for and integrates more information, considers more alternatives, and experiences a higher sense of urgency in changing the situation.

c) At a very high level of threat the person's ability to process information and perceive alternatives decreases. This can produce rigidity of positions and polarization of adversaries

Not only is the level of threat important, but the *direction of change* in the level of threat will combine with other factors to affect the productivity of dialogue at any point in time. For example, a brief period of high threat followed by a reduction of threat often leaves an after-image of the necessity for improvement and yet also currently provides a climate which allows for efficient information processing and exchange and behavioral change.

If the stress level is an important variable in the interpersonal system, what factors influence stress? The concept of decontrolling the conflict is useful here. One way that conflict can be decontrolled and the tension level increased is merely by increasing the parties' exposure to each other. Increasing exposure can involve bringing them face to face, reducing the number of other persons present, limiting their avenues of escape from each other, etc. A second way that tension can be increased is to instigate acts which sharpen the conflict issues between them, (for example, shifting the focus of dialogue from a symptomatic to a basic issue, or citing the consequences of a failure to agree). A third means for increasing tension is promoting the exchange of interpersonal reactions to each other. In emotional conflict, mutual recognition of their respective negative feelings is an instrumental step toward resolving the conflict, but adverse feedback contains a threat to one's self-esteem, and in turn is stressful.

The threat-stress-tension level can be purposefully reduced by control of the same factors above. These represent only a few illustrative factors which both influence the tension level and can in turn be influenced by the third party. The stress-inducing interventions can contribute to reaching an optimal level of stress in the system, but they can also cause a superoptimal level.

How did this function of tension management enter into the third-party role in our illustrative cases?

Throughout the Bill–Lloyd and Fred–Charles confrontations, Dave's interventions took into account the level of threat, stress, or tension. Encouraging them to share their negative perceptions and feelings certainly provided for temporarily increased tension. He also used or encouraged humor to reduce the general level of tension or to make a specific piece of threatening information more acceptable.

In the Mack—Sy case, the tension level tended to be quite high from the start. The conflict was intensely felt. For Mack, an especially sharp increase in the threat level probably occurred when he learned the purpose of the first meeting and then when his failure to join the issue brought additional pressure from all the parties present.

Dave had two alternative strategies for encouraging Mack to join the issues: (a) add pressure on Mack to force him into the arena, or (b) provide support for him so that he would feel secure enough to participate. Upon reflection after the episode, Dave concluded that he probably should have provided Mack with more active support, and that he should have tried harder to see the situation as Mack was seeing it. The point is that even before Dave added his own pressure, Mack probably was above, rather than below, the optimum tension level for productive dialogue.

The case also presents material bearing on the longer-run effect of a temporary period of high stress. Sy's outburst at the staff meeting both reflected the very high level of stress he felt and produced a high level of stress in others in the staff group. The stress level was undoubtedly superoptimal in terms of immediate utilization of the data produced by the confrontation. Yet the third party did not attempt to terminate the confrontation nor to tactically de-escalate it significantly. There were several factors supporting this choice, one of which was the assumption that the intense encounter and the after-images it created would lead to productive work subsequently. It did prove to be the climax which set the stage for the eventual improvements in the relationship.

The task of "tension management" after the intense confrontation changed somewhat in character. Tension needed to be reduced so that the parties could reflect upon and integrate the morning's experience. Tension reduction would be served if the principals—Mack and Sy—could gain at least indirect reassurance that other staff members did not disapprove of them as a result of the conflict, and if the other staff members could reassure themselves that the two adversaries were still intact after the morning confrontation. The fact that the staff group remained together and spent a prolonged lunch in rest and recuperation served these particular tension management needs.

SUMMARY

If well handled, the direct confrontation between participants can result in resolution or better control of the conflict. The third party can facilitate a productive confrontation by assessing and managing the following ingredients in the interaction setting: motivation, situational power, timing, pacing, tension level, communicative signs, and the group norms, process skills, and support relevant to openness.

7

THIRD-PARTY INTERVENTIONS
AND TACTICAL CHOICES

Having explored in Chapter 6 the broad strategic ingredients conducive to productive confrontation, the analysis now focuses on (a) preliminary interviewing, (b) the specific tactical choices involved in structuring the setting for a confrontation meeting, (c) the active interventions which facilitate the dialogue of the confrontation, and (d) the planning for further dialogue after the meeting.

PRELIMINARY INTERVIEWING

Preliminary one-on-one discussions between the potential third party and the conflict participants are usually valuable, and are sometimes essential. In the Fred—Charles case, the phone conversations with each person well in advance of the confrontation meeting provided Dave with essential information relative to their respective basic motivations and readiness to work on the conflict, the issues between them, the pressures operating on them, and their personal styles. In the Mack—Sy case, Dave had some relevant information. but not as much as he should have had, a point we have developed elsewhere. In the Bill—Lloyd case, Dave had only a brief and semiprivate interchange with Lloyd; the chat was used to get aquainted but not to discuss Lloyd's view of the conflict. While the confrontation worked out well, one could argue the desirability of more preliminary work. We will return to this point again in Chapter 8 in discussing the third party's role relationships with the principals.

The one-on-one discussions present the third party with an opportunity to develop the norms and skills favorable to openness and confrontation, and become a particularly important step when one or both of the principals involved have not had prior exposure to an experience along the lines of sensitivity training. The third party reported on here has developed the concepts and techniques of such interviews so that they are really temporary social systems with particular learning and developmental goals. The consultant has found that by treating seriously the learning possibilities of the one-on-one system, by providing substantial amounts of both challenge to and support for the clients, by furnishing the clients with an appropriate amount of feedback relevant to their immediate work and interactions, and by appropriate self-disclosures regarding his own ambivalences and uncertainties in the situation, he can provide the clients with experiences that substantially help prepare them for the confrontation they are contemplating. Through this preliminary session or sessions, a client often quickly and successfully experiences more openness than he would have expected, and develops some greater confidence that openness can be managed in ways that will increase his potency rather than his vulnerability.

In the next chapter, we will note the additional value of these interviews to the principals (as well as to the third party) in judging whether the third party might be helpful.

STRUCTURING THE CONTEXT FOR THE CONFRONTATION

Certain physical and social factors which provide the context for the confrontation can be influenced by the third party, in particular the neutrality of the territory, the formality of the setting, whether the encounter is time-bounded or open-ended, and the composition of the group in which the dialogue occurs.

Neutrality of the Turf

The site for the confrontation affects the balance of situational power. The condition of neutrality was literally met in the Mack–Sy case where the dialogue was initiated at the club, resumed at the staff meeting in the conference room, recapitulated at the club, and resumed at lunch during the consultant's second visit. As a contrast, the Bill—Lloyd confrontation occurred in Bill's large office. Nevertheless, the office was also frequently used for meetings even during Bill's absence and therefore, was relatively neutral territory. The same point applies to the personnel manager's office where Fred and Charles held their initial confrontation of differences. In both cases, comfortable chairs were used and neither home team sat at the personnel manager's desk (to have had anyone thus positioned would have created a significant asymmetry). If it is desirable to offset a power advantage of one party, one might do this by deliberately favoring the other in the selection of the confrontation site.

Formality of the Setting

The degree of formality of the setting should match the agenda, that is, the type of interpersonal work that needs to be accomplished. To illustrate, the Fred—Charles dialogue began in the office and then shifted to a much more casual setting—first a cocktail lounge and then a dining room. Although opposing considerations can undoubtedly be advanced, the following rationale supports the diversity and the sequence utilized in this case. In the office setting there is a greater sense of urgency to get on with whatever one is doing. This is helpful in identifying many of the conflicting views and feelings in a short period of time. By shifting to the restaurant and by adding one round of drinks, the interaction could become somewhat more relaxed, allowing for a mixture of social banter and direct work on the relationship. This sort of mixture often facilitates the more integrative and educative type of work which must follow the identification and clarification of the issues.

Another especially significant site choice—in terms of the formality consideration—was the director's decision to go to the club for lunch following the intensive confrontation between Mack and Sy. The relaxing atmosphere was most conducive to rest, recuperation and individual integration of the morning's experience.

Timeboundedness of the Encounter

The cases illustrate both inappropriate and appropriate time boundaries. For example, the amount of time available for the first meeting over cocktails turned out to be inadequate. The ending of the meeting was not natural. The group could have used more time. It was especially unfortunate that Mack was the only one who was available to go on, inasmuch as it was he who had not prepared for the nature of the meeting in the first place. In retrospect, the course of the episode might have been quite different if Dave had been prepared to cancel his other meetings, and urged Sy to reconsider leaving at that point. In any event, Dave could have productively spent more time with Mack, especially given Mack's comment in the car that the session was cut short.

Ambiguity about the time available for the dialogue and interruptions to the dialogue have potential effects which can be illustrated by reference to the Bill—Lloyd case. While there were no known time boundaries on the meeting, neither was there any understanding that a major part of the day could be devoted to the dialogue if that appeared to be desirable. Also, the dialogue was interrupted several times by Bill's secretary who was passing incoming phone calls on to him. The third party could have suggested that these phone calls be deferred to avoid interruption.

Open-endedness is especially important in the case of integrative and reconciliatory work. Thus, in the Mack—Sy case, it was just as important for the luncheon at the club to be open-ended as it was to be informal, in order for members individually and the group as a whole to assimilate and integrate the preceding events. Similarly, the reconciliation luncheon meeting between Mack and Sy was long and not time-bound—a fact essential to the work which was accomplished.

Another implication of the time perspective of the participants is its synchronizing effect. If both parties have a similar view of the time available for their interpersonal work, they are more likely to reciprocate each other's moves. For example, a person who assumes a relatively short time boundary is more likely to make à premature conciliatory overture—a bid to shift to the integrative phase before the other person has completed his differentiation initiatives.

Composition of the Meeting

The principals can work on their relationship by meeting alone, meeting with a third party, meeting with more than one third party, or meeting in the context of a larger group. Each person added has many potential effects: he may add relevant perceptions and insights; he may be perceived as a source of support; he may increase the feelings of risk of one or both principals if he is not trusted or if he is seen as having power over one or both of their respective careers; he may become identified as a third party for future work of the principals; and so on.

Several of these considerations are illustrated by the Fred—Charles case. At the outset the meeting involved the two principals and the third party, but later the group was enlarged to include the chief engineer.

Initially, the consultant preferred to work with only the two principals, to surface the issues in that smaller group. Recall that the earlier conflict incident related to the fifth-step grievance had occurred in the presence of several other persons. From their own reports, the audience had had an effect on both principals. Fred had felt embarrassed—apparently for over-exposing himself and for losing his objectivity. The effect of the audience on Charles had been very different. The presence of his boss and the chief engineer had *added* to his incentive to be confronting. It had provided him with a "fringe benefit," namely, the opportunity to prove that he was not always reserved and that he was willing to take risks. The consultant did not want Fred's participation in the dialogue—at least initially—to be inhibited or strictly objective; rather, he wanted each to feel free to express his feelings, his subjective views. Similarly, the consultant did not want Charles to be stimulated to be aggressive in order to impress another member of the staff. Therefore, it would have been a mistake to have included additional persons in this first phase.

The addition of the chief engineer in the second phase had a variety of potential effects. It added back one more element of the larger organizational reality, within which the two must ultimately work effectively. It had the potential of providing another source of emotional support and another source of perceptions of and reactions to the principals—data from which they might derive insight. There is always the risk that a fourth person also might inhibit one or both principals and/or complicate the system with another set of personal needs; however, in this case, because of the chief engineer's relationship to the parties and his direct interest in helping them, his entry into the continuation of the dialogue after work held more promise of gain than risk of disrupting the process.

Moreover, once the consultant had some base-line understanding of how Fred and Charles interacted without other members of the organization present, he could better detect the effects of others on Fred's and Charles' interaction patterns. If the consultant had had an opportunity to continue to work with Fred and Charles during the weeks following the confrontation, it would have been advisable to work with them in a group comprised of still more staff members.

In contrast with the above, the groupings in which Mack and Sy worked on their relationship were not always so appropriately composed. First, Dave chose to include the personnel manager as a fourth person in the *first* meeting of the principals. His primary purpose was to help build an internal third-party role for this person, but he did not consult the principals. As it turned out there were neither any short-term nor long-term advantages to including the personnel manager; his presence might have been an inhibiting factor.

The second encounter between Mack and Sy occurred in the staff group in the presence of their superior and their organizational peers. This composition probably increased the perceived risks more than it added to the potential either for relevant data or for support. While Dave could not have actively prevented Sy's outburst, he could have interrupted the interchange immediately after Sy's explanatory comments and suggested that the matter be pursued later in a smaller group. However, this intervention (which Dave did not even consider at the time) would have reduced the spontaneity of the interchange; it would have made everyone—principals and other staff members alike—more, rather than less, anxious; moreover, for better or for worse the matter was now a group as well as an interpersonal problem.

An important composition decision was made when the staff meeting broke for lunch after the intensive morning session. Dave actively sought to keep the group intact in order to allow members to provide each other with reassurances and to gradually reduce the general level of anxiety of members of the staff. In addition, as it turned out, it was useful to have all members of the staff present during the discussion initiated by Mack about Dave's role.

During his second visit, Dave appropriately limited the meeting to Mack and Sy. He didn't know what would happen. He only sensed that there was the potential for constructive work. Dave later concluded that if another person had been present, Mack would not have been as willing to make the same self-disclosures, which provided both the symbolic overture and the information that were the bases for reconciliation.

The fact that Sy and Mack did not work on their relationship during the period between Dave's two visits suggests that in this case the two principals themselves needed a third party for them to work productively. This would be especially true in cases where the principals' interpersonal styles are a source of, or confounding factor in, the conflict.

INTERVENTIONS THAT FACILITATE THE DIALOGUE PROCESS

At various points in these three cases the third party played an active role in influencing both the content and the nature of the process of the dialogue: he refereed the interaction process, initiated agenda, restated issues and views, elicited reactions, and offered his own observations. These third-party interventions are illustrated by analysis of the Fred–Charles case. The third party also diagnosed the conflict, prescribed the discussion method, diagnosed conditions causing poor dialogue, and made other counseling interventions before, during, and after the confrontation meetings. The Mack–Sy case will be analyzed to illustrate these interventions.

Refereeing the Interaction Process

The third party can play an active role in regulating certain aspects of the process. For example, on several occasions in the Fred–Charles case, he terminated a discussion which had become either repetitive or counterproductive. On other occasions in the same episode, he played an active role in providing for equal time, and for shorter, more frequent interchanges. Rather than let a person go on at some length and introduce several ideas, he would try to allow the other to respond immediately to a point already made by the first person.

The third party may choose to make limited use of rewards and punishment in refereeing the process. Although not always as a result of explicit choices, Dave sometimes sanctioned principals' behavior. As an example of a reward, Charles probably felt gratified when Dave and Fred (at Dave's inducement) differentiated Charles' "genuine regret" from his "false humility." During another interchange, Dave glowered at Charles, presumably to punish him for trying to use Dave's suggestion to his own advantage and put Fred down.

Initiating Agenda

The third party can play an active role in determining the foci of the principals' discussions. As an illustration, the first interchange between Fred and Charles was focused on the task disagreement which had been identified in the staff meeting.

This topic provided a conflict interchange which did not require a third party to play an active role until he better understood how they related to each other. Also, Dave was confident that the discussion would reflect some general relationship problems, as it actually proved to do. This and a second "agenda" item were clearly determined by the third party. Each was systematically pursued at some length.

Third-party initiative in explicitly setting agenda is usually most needed early in the meeting. Therefore, later in the Fred–Charles meeting, as the dialogue developed its own momentum, the focus of discussion shifted more rapidly and was influenced by all participants. The consultant's interjections—that is, his observations, reactions, and requests for other's reactions—became more frequent and continued to sharply influence the focus of discussion, but often only to make a particular point.

A qualification to the pattern of declining third-party initiative in setting agenda occurs when the differentiation phase has run its course, and integrative agenda are appropriate. The third party can often synchronize this transition by again being active, explicitly stating appropriate agenda.

Restating the Issue and the Principals' Views

One of the most frequent third-party interventions in interpersonal conflict is an attempt to summarize each party's views—concerns or preferences—as heard by the third party. Dave frequently contributed such a summary, and then checked to see whether the person was satisfied with his statement. This was noted in the previous chapter, where the intervention was shown to help improve the reliability of communication. In addition, we can note here that these restatements sometimes were an effective way of terminating a discussion, particularly in the Fred—Charles case. Their summary quality not only gave closure to a particular discussion, but when the discussion had become a debate, it also reduced the importance of issues of "face," such as which of the principals would have the last word.

Sometimes the third party's restatement constituted a redefinition of the issue in a more general form. For example, the question of whether management should make a tentative scheduling decision before or after Charles had contacted Corporate Personnel was translated into their differing jurisdictional concepts. To have reached agreement on the specific decision, which happened to be of little practical import, would not have constituted progress in resolving the more basic issues underlying the conflict.

Eliciting Reactions and Offering Observations

Another very common third-party intervention takes the form of encouraging an interpersonal communication process sometimes referred to as "feedback " For example, early in the process between Fred and

Charles, the two principals exchanged the interpersonal perceptions which they had developed. Their behavior toward each other had been, and continued to be, governed in part by these perceptions. Therefore, sharing these descriptions gave each a better understanding of how he was perceived by and reacted to by the other. In addition to asking the principals to share an initial inventory of perceptions, Dave encouraged the *three* of them to try to identify and understand the patterns in their current interactions and to share their current perceptions of, and emotional reactions to, each other.

The account of the Fred–Charles confrontation included instances where a person received "feedback" that may have yielded him new insight. For example, Fred appeared to gain insight into his tendency to be "feisty," to "lecture," and to bypass or exclude Charles. Also, Charles gained a new appreciation of his own tendency to use cross-examination techniques and to "pile on" when an adversary is being confronted by another person. The timing of such bits of "feedback" as these is important. Ideally they are given when they relate to some recent behavior and can also be heard by the principal involved.

Diagnosing the Conflict

The third party can emplicitly focus the group's attention on diagnosis. The Mack–Sy case illustrates various types of interventions that generate or test diagnostic hunches.

First, during his session with Sy, Dave encouraged Sy to sharpen his own insights regarding his feelings toward Mack. Dave's task was to question and listen. Dave then tried to get Sy to identify what irritants he himself brought to the relationship. To sharpen the issue Dave described for Sy his own positive reaction to Mack. Dave invited Sy to try to state his hunches about his most central concern with Mack.

Second, during the staff-meeting encounter, Dave spelled out two alternate views of Mack's behavior: either as attempts to prove the mismatch between himself and his controller job, or as attempts to minimize the mismatch. If Mack were viewed as trying to highlight the mismatch, presumably this would be a self-defeating pattern in terms of Mack's career. Therefore, Dave believed Mack should know what impressions he was creating, and have an opportunity to re-evaluate his own current behavior. Sy confirmed that he did see Mack as trying to prove the mismatch. Others might have been invited to offer their perceptions but only at the risk of creating too much pressure on Mack. Instead

Dave invited Mack to consider the possibility that his behavior pointed to that conclusion, even though he didn't consciously have that intention.

Third, during the rest and recuperation session, Dave offered his own assessment that Sy would not use this confrontation against Mack in the future, an assessment at variance with what Mack feared. It is not clear whether Mack was persuaded at the time. Nevertheless, Mack's self-disclosures in the reconciliation session suggest that he eventually developed confidence in Sy's integrity and self-discipline—before he had developed any personal rapport with him.

Other aspects of the Mack—Sy conflict were not, but perhaps should have been, explicitly diagnosed by the principals and the third party. For example, they might have tried to achieve understanding of what events in the staff meeting had triggered Sy. As Chapter 5 emphasized, if the persons involved understand the triggering events, they can develop some relatively operational means for controlling the conflict in the future.

Another aspect of all three cases which could have been diagnosed were the pressures and uncertainties which existed in the work environment and added to the current tension among the members. The third party might have tested how various persons assessed these factors and whether they were impinging on members differently. Clearly, Mack's sense of the real possibility of organization failure in his case may have been sharpened by the recent setbacks of two members of the staff. The up-or-out character of his current organizational position made realistic his interest in looking for alternate jobs.

Prescribing Discussion Methods

The third party can prescribe discussion techniques that assist the parties in joining the issues and engaging each other more directly.

For example, during the first encounter at cocktails in the Mack—Sy case, Dave asked Mack to show the relationship between his own personal problems upon which he had just elaborated, on the one hand, and his feelings about Sy on the other. Such a request regarding relevance often gives the person himself a new insight into the issues, as well as giving the other person a way of responding. In this case, Mack declined at least in part because he was not ready to confront Sy.

Dave made a related type of intervention with Sy. Sy had just asked Mack to suggest the bases of his, Sy's, negative feelings. The third party noted that this was not a productive way to join the issue, and urged Sy himself to provide the historical *data* of the events, incidents, etc., on which his feelings were based. Sy's subsequent statements became more helpful in clarifying his feelings, the patterns of Mack's behavior which contributed to these feelings, and Sy's resultant reactions.

In the discussion which followed, Dave allowed the principals to surface many of the points of friction (without elaborating them), hoping there would be a dominant theme, and also wanting to see where the pair was headed. An alternative would have been to work on any one issue more thoroughly—for example, to try to get the principals to identify the practical differences involved.

Diagnosing Conditions Causing Poor Dialogue

Often, the reason for poor dialogue cannot be remedied by prescribing dialogue techniques. The third party must help identify more basic attitudes or other reality factors that are limiting the prospects for productive dialogue. The Mack—Sy case provides illustrations.

In the first encounter, Dave identified and stressed the difficulty inherent in Mack's statement, "That is how I am." Mack communicated the attitude that there is no room for negotiation—either compromise or integrative problem-solving. It later occurred to Dave that he might have gone further and said to Mack, "Yes, that is how you feel right now as things stand. What condition would have to change, including those under Sy's control, that would allow you to feel differently?"

Throughout the first two encounters, Dave had gained a growing impression that the major difficulty in achieving any progress in the relationship was the imbalance between Sy's initiative in getting the issues out and Mack's reluctance to either join the issues or show interest in improving the relationship. By identifying Sy's admitted dependence on Mack and Mack's denial of dependence on Sy, he underscored this as a roadblock, and subtly indicated that it might be wise to back off until Mack communicated direct dependence on Sy and thereby defined the situation more symmetrically.

Another attitude displayed by Mack which had the effect of limiting the prospect of fruitful dialogue was his concern about the future risks for him, especially if Sy became his boss. Dave missed an opportunity to work with Mack on this issue early in the first meeting. Had Mack been encouraged to elaborate when he mentioned his concern about working for Sy, this not only would have achieved more symmetrical initiative in the dialogue, and further engaged the principals, but might have given Mack a chance to discuss the risks he believed he was taking in treating the problem right then.

Other Counseling Interventions

Although many of the same interventions have been analyzed in terms of the specific functions they perform, we note here several different types of counsel that can be offered the principals: advice about the appropriate timing for interpersonal confrontation; suggestions as to realistic expectations about the progress which can be achieved in the relationship; urging colleagues of the principals to contribute in ways that are available to them.

A more direct form of counsel is illustrated by Dave's response to Mack's desire for some techniques that might better enable him to change the pattern of his relations with others. He gave specific counsel, drawing upon experience with other persons with whom he had worked in the past. In contrast, he failed to counsel Sy in this way, despite the fact that Sy also expressed some feeling of inadequacy in working on interpersonal issues. Dave had regarded Sy's behavior as adequate, and he himself was pressed for time; therefore, he didn't explore these feelings of Sy's. Given the fact that Sy subsequently avoided encounters with Mack during the period between Dave's visits, Dave missed an important cue here.

PLANNING FOR FUTURE DIALOGUE

Generally the dialogue experience itself will increase the principals' capacity to continue to pursue their conflict constructively, especially if they develop some rapport and are reinforced by their efforts at openness. However, there are several steps a third party can take to improve the effectiveness of continuing work when he won't be around. The case studies contained instances where the consultant failed to take advantage of all the opportunities identified in subsequent analysis.

First, the general organization climate—apart from the immediate conflict—is important. Several elements of the climate of the organizations studied are relevant. For example, in the Mack–Sy case there was an explicit norm that the staff would be open about its conflicts and there was a legitimacy to analyzing their own group process. The director's own behavior patterns reinforced these two tendencies in his subordinates. Finally, his interest in management development increased a manager's tendency to confront in a conflict because even if the relationship didn't improve, the experience could be educational. In that sense there was less chance for complete "failure."

The influence between organizational climate and these interpersonal confrontations was two-way. For example, by identifying, emphasizing, and conceptualizing lateral relations in the Mack–Sy case, the consultant increased the salience of this dimension of that organization. As noted above, the director had provided a general climate in which there was encouragement for his managers to explicitly appraise relationships and work toward their improvement, but he almost exclusively attended to vertical relations between himself and subordinates. Dave's responsiveness to difficulties experienced in lateral relations complemented the director's orientation. The work with Sy and Mack provided both a rough model and also an impetus for other staff members to work on their lateral relationships.

Second, the practice with constructive dialogue techniques during their meetings with the consultant should have increased the principals' ability to use them on their own, especially if these techniques or principles were made explicit and stated in operational terms. It is possible for a third party to stimulate productive dialogue content and also to manage the interaction in a way which provides greater understanding about the conflict in question but does not ensure that the principals themselves learn what the ingredients were which make the dialogue constructive. For example, in the Fred–Charles case, the consultant merely terminated and derived some essential points from a discussion which had degenerated into an exchange of personal attacks. He missed an opportunity to lead the three of them into a discussion of the destructiveness of that type of interchange and a diagnosis of how it got started and was perpetuated. Such a group diagnosis might have resulted in the development of methods by which the principals could avoid ego-bruising interchanges in the future. The consultant did endeavor to achieve this kind of insight into one aspect of the process when he asked the principals to consider how they could in the future better avoid the rejection that develops when one (especially Charles) makes a positive overture that the other does not feel like reciprocating.

Third, the consultant can attempt to build another third party into the process—one who will be more readily available to the principals than is the outside consultant. Involving the chief engineer in the Fred–Charles case met this future-oriented need and constituted an asset for the immediate confrontation. Dave urged the two principals to view the engineer in this way. In the case of Mack and Sy the personnel manager was purposely involved, but he did not have a sustained interest in this kind of role, and consequently didn't perform this function.

Fourth, it would have been helpful if Dave had been *available* to these three pairs over the next few weeks following the confrontation. This is especially relevant for the Mack–Sy case, considering Sy's inhibition about working alone with Mack on their relationship. On the other hand, it may have been best for Mack to shift his attention to his relationship with the director, even if that meant "putting on ice" his conflictful relationship with Sy.

Fifth, the third party can ensure that the principals have a specific time and/or purpose planned for getting together again. In the Bill–Lloyd case, an explicit decision was made by the parties to take some action steps; the third party received periodic reports and nothing more seemed to be required. In the Mack–Sy case no such specific plan emerged from the first meeting at cocktails. If another meeting had been planned, Sy might have felt more choice between confronting Mack in the staff group in the morning or in the other session planned for later. Also, the principals had not agreed upon any plan for meeting again at the time the consultant departed, with the result that Mack's initiations were not reciprocated and no meetings occurred between the consultant's visits. Similarly, in the Fred–Charles case the consultant did not ensure that the principals had made explicit plans to follow up on their confrontation meeting.

SUMMARY

In this chapter we have analyzed and arrayed the many tactical interventions which perform the third-party functions set forth in the previous chapter.

Various aspects of the setting for a confrontation are both relevant to strategic ingredients of a confrontation and amenable to influence by the third party, including the neutrality of the territory, the formality versus the informality of the setting, the time boundaries of the meeting, and the composition of the group in which the dialogue occurs.

Innumerable possibilities exist for tactical interventions into the on-going process. They fall into the following categories: refereeing the interaction process, suggesting agenda, clarifying participants' messages, eliciting and offering interpersonal feedback, diagnosing the conflict issues, prescribing discussion methods, diagnosing difficulties in the dialogue process, and counseling.

Planning and preparation for further dialogue after the meeting will be facilitated if the third party actually attempts to teach the parties about the functions and techniques which have already facilitated or could potentially facilitate their dialogue. Ideally, either he or someone else whom he has already built into the process will be available for future third-party work with the pair if necessary. It is very important for the third party to ensure that the principals have agreed in relatively specific terms to meet again and continue their work.

8

THIRD-PARTY ATTRIBUTES

What attributes of the third party and of his relations with the principals influence his ability to perform the strategic functions and implement the tactical interventions described above? What problems are frequently encountered in establishing and maintaining the appropriate third-party role? This chapter analyzes the case studies for the insight they yield into the above questions. Inasmuch as all three cases involve an outside consultant in the third-party role, the chapter will extend the analysis to an examination of the potential for organizational peers, superiors, and staff personnel to perform useful third-party functions.

ESTABLISHING AND MAINTAINING APPROPRIATE ROLE

Establishing Professional Expertise and Personal Qualities

The professional and personal qualities attributed to the third party which give the principals confidence in entering a confrontation and which facilitate confrontation processes include (a) diagnostic skill, (b) behavioral skills in breaking impasses and interrupting repetitive interchange, (c) attitudes of acceptance, and (d) a personal capacity to provide emotional support and reassurance.

In the introduction to this report we described how the third-party consultant was viewed by all three pairs of principals. His professional identity with sensitivity training and the principals' prior experience with that type of training combined to make it relatively easier for the consultant to be seen as a person who could facilitate an interpersonal confrontation. Beyond that, he had in fact demonstrated some consulting skill in other projects within each of these organizations, projects which themselves did not necessarily require the same level of trust and confidence that one must invest in a consultant in seeking his assistance as a third party to an intensive interpersonal conflict.

As a result, in the cases studied here the third party had to engage in very little "face-work" or other preliminary activities in establishing his role and his competence and in communicating the attitudes which support a successful confrontation. In other situations, this effort to establish the appropriate role identity and personal attributes may be a significant part of the third party's total job in assisting two parties in conflict.

Where the potential third party has not had any prior role relationships with the principals to the conflict, one-on-one discussions between the third person and each principal are used as a basis for judging the likelihood that the third person could make a positive contribution in a confrontation.

Establishing Appropriate Power and Knowledge

The perceived power of the third party and his general knowledge of the principals, issues, and background factors are important attributes.

It is an advantage for the third party to have little or no power over the futures of the principals. This type of third-party power increases the participants' sense of risk in confronting issues candidly and/or is likely to induce them to behave in ways which are calculated to elicit the approval of the third party. For example, the mere presence of Charles' and Fred's boss (even though he was not trying to perform third-party functions) helped shape their interaction with each other in an encounter prior to their confrontation session.

In the three cases studied, the third party was an outside consultant with no formal power over the payoffs or careers of the participants. However, in each case he had a close relationship with the principals' superior. Therefore, despite the consultant's efforts to preserve a non-evaluative stance toward organizational members and to preserve the confidentiality of all of his separate relationships, it seems reasonable to believe that participants perceived at least slight potential advantage in presenting their preferred image to the consultant.

In one of the three cases this issue was sharpened for the consultant when he later discovered that Charles' termination was linked in the minds of some organizational members with the confrontation between Charles and Fred in which he was involved as a third party.

Another type of power is an asset to the third party, namely, control over aspects of the process. The advantage of control of certain factors is obvious from our discussion of the importance of setting, composition of group, agenda, phasing, etc. Of course, the perceived expertise of the third party usually is responded to by a willingness to accept his direction in these areas, but it is often helpful to him to have effective control over these dimensions of the situation even before he has fully established himself with the particular principals in conflict.

At least moderate knowledge of the principals, issues, and background factors usually is an advantage. It not only enhances the third party's credibility with the principals, but also increases the likelihood that his interventions will be on target.

The prior knowledge reduces the amount of time which the principals spend talking to the third party rather than each other (this admittedly is not always an advantage). One factor arguing against a third party's being highly knowledgeable about the issues and persons involved is that it is harder for the principals to believe he does not have his own opinions, about either the issues or the person's views, which disqualify him as a disinterested party.

Establishing Neutrality

Differences in the third party's relationships to the two principals can influence his effectiveness. Three different types of third-party symmetry are important: Is he neutral with respect to outcome? Is he equally close to or distant from the parties in a sociometric sense? Does he avoid ground rules for handling differences which would inadvertently operate to the advantage of one and the disadvantage of the other? Symmetry is usually helpful, but not always necessary. Actually in some cases, asymmetrical third-party roles or interventions are more effective (e.g., when they offset a basic power or skill asymmetry between the parties themselves). The discussion here calls attention to the importance of this role attribute and analyzes this dimension of each of the three episodes.

First, it is usually important for a third-party consultant to be neutral regarding the substantive positions of the parties and the outcome. This could have become an issue in the Bill–Lloyd case because of Dave's prior association with an issue in the conflict; Dave had participated in the team-building session that created the open, fluid pattern of group functioning which Bill wanted to preserve and Lloyd said he wanted to change. However, in fact, as the confrontation unfolded, Dave felt as sympathetic to Lloyd as to Bill. For example, it seemed perfectly appropriate to Dave that Bill agree to reconsider the operating pattern of the group, taking into account Lloyd's preferences. Also, Lloyd's demands at the intergroup level seemed to him to be legitimate and deserving of response.

Maintaining neutrality regarding the substantive issues often requires that the third party detect and deflect bids by one principal to include him in a coalition against the other principal. This is illustrated in the case where Dave had to be alert to avoid having his own confronting behavior toward Fred used by Charles as if Dave and Charles were allies. At one point, Dave explicitly dissociated himself from Charles.

Second, it is usually best for the third party to be comparably related to the principals in a personal sense. Only the Fred–Charles case illustrates this ideal. The consultant's short-term relationships with both persons were friendly, but professional. Dave had information about the parties and also some assurance of the esteem with which he was held and the type of consultant-role identity they attributed to him. Both Fred and Charles had mentioned the possibility of gaining Dave's active third-party assistance during his next visit. Reciprocally, Dave had demonstrated his interest in and concern for each of them during long phone conversations in which the principals had each ventilated feelings and tried to gain new perspective on their conflict. Therefore, there was no general problem in achieving a neutral identity and relatively satisfactory role relationship with the principals.

The third party was asymmetrically close to Bill at the outset of the latter's confrontation with Lloyd. Dave's considerable prior consulting relationship with Bill made it impossible for him in a short period of time to become similarly related to Lloyd—in terms of warmth, personal respect, trust, and general familiarity. Nevertheless, Dave probably should have sought a way to spend more time with Lloyd before the confrontation in order to reduce this type of asymmetry. As it happened, this initial asymmetry did not interfere with the consultant's effectiveness. Why? Apparently because Lloyd attached more importance to Dave's professional identity than his personal relations with the principals. Some time after the confrontation, Lloyd said,

> Yes, I recognized that Dave was closer to Bill and the group, but I didn't assume he was therefore biased. This gets into professionalism. I assume that Dave, in his professional role, has his own built-in gyros keeping him neutral. Sure he confronted me about some of my behavior and made me uncomfortable, but he couldn't be a dish rag and still be effective, either.

There was moderate asymmetry in his personal relations with Mack and Sy, Dave initially being somewhat closer to Sy. Dave had an open and high mutual trust relationship with Sy throughout the entire period of this episode. Also, in his initial encounters with Mack, Dave had responded favorably to Mack's intensity and his desire to learn more about himself. He assumed that Mack felt closer to him as a result of sharing the emotionally significant lab experience and receiving Dave's own sympathetic, confirming responses. However, Dave had spent relatively little time with Mack prior to the beginning of this episode, and had had little time to build up mutual confidence. Also, Mack's choice not to identify the person toward whom he felt intense conflict could have been a signal of the qualified nature of his relationship with Dave. Nevertheless, it is doubtful that this asymmetry in prior contact was responsible for Mack's ambivalent feelings toward Dave and the confrontation, feelings which became apparent later. This brings us to a consideration of the third type of symmetry which did figure importantly in the Mack–Sy case, namely, whether the consultant's methods in general and tactical interventions in particular tend to favor either one of the principals.

The Bill–Lloyd case illustrates how the third party's approach can be differentially favored by the principals. The norms of openness, acceptance, emotional support, analysis of group process, etc., which the consultant passively (by his identity and presence) and actively (by his interventions) brought to the confrontation were those Bill favored. Considering Lloyd's relative concern about excessive "groupiness" in the larger task group and also Dave's earlier hunch that Lloyd might tend to resist dealing with the more emotional aspects of issues, one might have expected him to either resent or resist the consultant's methodology. As it turned out he participated fully, utilizing the process to get his own views and concerns out in a forceful way. Moreover, the process was general enough to allow him to utilize bargaining behavior (e.g., to hint at contingent actions if the two of them could not reach agreement).

Inasmuch as the consultant's own methodological model also incorporated that form of interpersonal conflict resolution, he made no attempt to reprove Lloyd for those departures from a conciliatory problem-solving approach. Thus, the potential disadvantage to Lloyd did not materialize.

The tactical asymmetries which occurred in the Mack—Sy case did have adverse consequences for the confrontation. Dave's actions prior to the confrontation allowed Sy to participate in the decision whether to meet with Mack to work on their relationship, but did not even ensure that Mack was informed of the purpose of the meeting at cocktails. Clearly, for reasons we have analyzed in detail in earlier chapters, this placed Mack at a disadvantage and led to his feelings that the confrontation had been "rigged." In addition, the nature of Dave's interventions may have seemed one-sided to Mack. Because Dave was trying to get the parties engaged in a direct dialogue and because Sy was currently more ready than Mack to confront their differences, Dave actually had to put more pressure on Mack than on Sy.

If basic trust in the third party is high, it is less costly for him to give asymmetrical support to one party's ideas, perceptions, feelings, and actions. He is less likely to be seen by either party as having negative intentions toward the party to whom the consultant gives less support or whom he actively opposes. In fact, where the consultant has a much better relationship with one party, he is better able to confront that party forcefully and introduce content threatening to that party. He also is better able to make interventions that interrupt, interfere with that person's present approach, or place restrictive ground rules on that person (like "keep quiet and listen" or "would you try to state what you heard him say").

Improving a Deteriorating Relationship

Improving a deteriorating relationship between the third party and a principal requires a conscious effort on the former's part. The Mack—Sy case provides some insight into the processes involved.

It was only after the second confrontation meeting that Dave learned about Mack's perceptions that the first meeting had been "rigged" and how Mack's feelings of trust toward Dave had suffered accordingly. It is unclear just when Mack had developed those feelings toward Dave, but Dave's effectiveness with Mack would have been limited from that point on. It now becomes clear that Dave had missed an important and timely opportunity to actively encourage Mack to raise such an issue when Mack drove Dave back to the motel after cocktails.

The circumstances under which Mack finally did state his feelings about Dave are significant. Mack's comments followed Dave's expression of his own irritation with another person, the personnel manager. By expressing personal negative feelings he became more available as a target for other persons' irritation, rather than wholly protected by his professional role.

Mack's perceptions and feelings were of immediate concern to Dave. Dave wanted to be understood: if he had not maintained Mack's confidence it was through an omission in judgment, not some lack of identification with Mack. Dave's efforts to repair his relationship with Mack included the following:

a) Dave explained the steps involved in the decision and objected to the label or interpretation "rigged";

b) he humorously claimed his good intentions, by saying that he had been operating under the assumption that he was seen as wearing a "white hat";

c) he directly reflected the importance of the issue to him, by emphasizing how crucial trust is to his role in the group;

d) he stressed and recounted his positive feelings for Mack, which he related to Sy the day before;

e) later, in touching base with Mack before departing, Dave expressed the positive feelings and concern he had for Mack by indicating that he liked Mack, that the two of them were similar, and that he was available if Mack needed him.

Dave felt more positive toward Mack than the latter seemed to sense. At the same time, he appreciated that he had not acted as clearly on Mack's views, preferences and concerns as he had on Sy's in arranging for the two of them to work on their relationship. Mack's feelings toward Dave, as expressed at the club, were ambivalent. His negative feelings toward Dave were partly related to his feelings of vulnerability to Sy. He believed he could be hurt by what had happened between himself and Sy. He also had some positive feelings—that the experience had present or potential learning value for him. As he said, he had wanted more candid reaction to him from his group at the sensitivity-training laboratory he had attended.

Evidently after Mack's expression of his feelings to Dave and the dialogue that ensued with Dave, his feelings toward Dave improved. For example, he expressed a desire to work further with Dave. The phone conversations he initiated with Dave also reflected growing trust and confidence. Finally, the visit during which the reconciliation occurred confirmed that they had developed a close, trusting relationship.

INTERNAL CONSULTANTS, ORGANIZATIONAL PEERS AND SUPERIORS AS THIRD PARTIES

That concerned members of an organization experience frustration in having to rely upon external consultants for skilled third parties and that there is a need for organizations to devise ways to make such resources available in the right place and time and in the right role is argued as follows by Richard Barrett, director, Management Systems Staff, Bureau of the Budget, in his published comments on the Bill and Lloyd case:

> ... success in this case resulted from the longitudinal nature of the organizational development effort. I hear a great deal of talk about the importance of "follow up" but, like "research," I don't see it happening very often. This case, I think, is a fine illustration of the kinds of pay-off that can be achieved by having a competent "third party" available at the right time. Too often, it seems to me, we lose ball games in the late innings simply because we do not have the right man in the right spot at the right time. It is clear in this instance that the confrontation between Bill and Lloyd would not have taken place if Dave had not (a) been present in the immediate work environment at the time the two men were experiencing difficulties, and (b) already established some degree of rapport with the two individuals involved. The fact that this is one of two or three instances when this happy set of circumstances occurred during the course of the organizational development effort described in the case poses a considerable problem for others engaged in organizational development activities. That it did not happen more often in our situation is explained principally by our almost complete dependence on outside consultants to perform third-party roles. Of necessity, the work of these individuals was sporadic and tended to be focused on predetermined tasks and projects. Their availability for on-the-job third-party consultation was therefore accidental. One solution to this problem might have been to give the consultants more free time to rove through the organization looking for "hang-ups" and to encourage their attendance in staff meetings and other group

meetings. A second possibility is, of course, the development of internal resources. While we had some success with this approach, we found it difficult to create an image of employees as true third parties.[1]

An outside consultant may be in the best overall position to operate effectively as a third party. Nevertheless, organizational members potentially can play important third-party roles. Figure 8-1 depicts the several types of organizational role relationships considered here.

On the basis of our discussion earlier in this chapter, we propose five role attributes for identifying potential third parties from within an organization and for judging the potential effectiveness of persons who would be third parties:

1. high professional expertise regarding social processes;
2. low power over fate of principals;
3. high control over confrontation setting and processes;
4. moderate knowledge about the principals, issues, and background factors;
5. neutrality or balance with respect to substantive outcome, personal relationships, and conflict-resolution methodology.

There is a growing practice for large organizations to provide organizational consulting as a service supplied by the personnel department or some separate staff unit. How well do internal organizational consultants usually match these requisite role attributes? They frequently are seen as possessing sufficient professional expertise although not as much as is attributed to the outside consultant. This edge in expertise held by the external consultant may be offset by the advantage of the internal consultant's more continuous availability. Internals are more likely than are the outside consultants to be regarded as having an optimum amount of background knowledge. They usually can acquire sufficient control over the setting and process. However, the internals encounter moderately more difficulty than externals in demonstrating low power over the future of the principals and in achieving perceived neutrality.

Organizational peers who have an interest in, but no formal responsibility for, performing third-party functions are at a greater

---

[1] Barrett, R. "Comments on the Preceding Article." *J. Appl. Behav. Sci.* **4**, (3), pp. 346–347

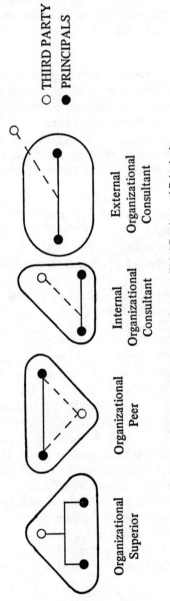

Figure 8-1. Role Relationships between Third Parties and Principals

○ THIRD PARTY
● PRINCIPALS

Organizational Superior

Organizational Peer

Internal Organizational Consultant

External Organizational Consultant

disadvantage than are internal consultants. Typically, it is more difficult for them to establish the requisite professional expertise and neutrality and to gain sufficient control over the setting and process. Moreover, they are often perceived as having superoptimal knowledge about the principals, issues, and background factors.

·· Organizational superiors are operating under the greatest handicap, even if they are perceived as having high professional expertise and do have high control over process. They tend to have high power and superoptimal knowledge, and it is difficult for them to establish neutrality.

The above are general tendencies—one would expect to find considerable variation among persons within each class of organizational role as well as among outside consultants.

BEING ONESELF

We have attempted to develop a general third-party theory and to outline generally applicable third-party practices. If anything, we have been *too* successful in being objective in describing Dave's tactics, his functions, and his more obvious role attributes. It must be acknowledged that the acceptance of Dave as a third party and the impact of his third-party interventions were conditioned by such personal attributes and patterns as the following: he manifested a predilection for confrontation in his own encounters with others; he had a high energy level which sometimes had the effect of energizing the process; his changeable moods from extreme patience to impatience and abruptness were sometimes consistent and sometimes inconsistent with the needs of the situation; he had a high need to achieve an analytical understanding of what was happening, which was combined with a tendency to be emotionally moved with concern and empathy for a person struggling to express himself, to articulate his feelings, and to engage another; he occasionally was anxious about whether the confrontation would help or hurt the relationship, and whether or not his interventions would facilitate the confrontation; and so on.

While it is *not* important for the general theory or general practice to incorporate these aspects of Dave's personal style or the way he comes across to others, these factors probably would have to be taken into account if one were to more fully understand what happened in these three or any other other specific cases. Moreover, it *is* important for the general theory and practice to know that such personal attributes and styles do condition the role and the interventions of the person; his personal attributes must fit what he is trying to do in a third-party (or in any other) sociotherapist role. Perhaps the most significant point to make here is that, at least in the case of Dave, his approach was not to try to suppress his personal self or to subordinate it to some ideal professional role to any great extent, but rather to act on his own feelings and intuition, knowing full well that he would express something about himself as well as perform essential functions, and just to assume that his batting average would continue to be good.

9

SUMMARY AND CONCLUSIONS

This book is intended to increase our understanding of interpersonal conflict, to contribute to a theory of third-party interventions, to improve the practice of organizational consultation, and to stimulate client systems to consider how they might utilize third parties, especially in connection with other organizational development activities.

We have presented three case histories of interpersonal conflict and the interventions of a third-party consultant. These case histories provided some of the empirical basis for constructing a middle-range theory of a form of sociotherapy. The chain of reasoning employed in developing the subject matter runs along the following lines: First, we proposed a diagnostic model which identified several aspects of a conflict cycle that make conflict subject to controls—controls which may be utilized with or without the parties' directly confronting each other. Second, we postulated the potential gains and risks that accompany the use of direct confrontations. Then, taking cognizance of this mixed potential from direct confrontations we hypothesized factors that enhance the likelihood of successful confrontations. These factors were used to define the strategic functions of third parties, which also gave meaning to our subsequent treatment of the tactical interventions of third parties. In the chapter on third-party role attributes, we extended the inference process to the next step. Given the tactics he must execute, and the functions he must perform, we determined which role attributes facilitate the work of the third party.

ASPECTS OF INTERPERSONAL CONFLICT AND THEIR IMPLICATIONS

Chapter 5 presented our diagnostic model of interpersonal-conflict episodes involving four basic elements—issues, triggering events, conflict, or conflict-resolving acts of the principals, and their consequences. The model incorporates the ideas that interpersonal conflicts are cyclical (they follow cycles of manifestation and latency) and that they are dynamic (they change from one cycle to the next).

Malevolent cycling was shown to result from the *tendency for issues to proliferate:* First, a person in a conflictful relationship will often introduce new issues for various tactical reasons. Second, a person's acts pursuant to the current issues in contention often inadvertently produce new antagonisms. Third, one's way of coping with the consequences of conflict may actually exacerbate, rather than minimize, the conflict. (For example, a person may choose to withdraw or avoid encounters out of fear or in order to conserve emotional energy. If the second person is dependent on the first or tries to confront their conflict, the first's coping strategy of avoidance will turn out to create additional issues for the second.)

Examined again in light of a subsequent chapter treating the direct confrontation, the risk of malevolent cycling also can be seen as deriving from several conditions which affect *the tendency for conflict resolution moves to be nonreciprocal*: asymmetrical motivation and situational power, poor synchronization, overall imbalance in the differentiation and integration activities or poor sequencing of them, inadequate support for openness, inadequate dialogue language, and suboptimal or superoptimal tension. More on these general factors later.

Let us return to a review of Chapter 5 where we proposed that a general operational objective of conflict management was to interrupt self-maintaining and malevolent cycles, achieve a de-escalation of the conflict, and initiate a benevolent cycling of the conflict. In particular, the chapter explores how each of several elements of a conflict episode presents one or more "handles" for controlling conflict.

If one understands the types of events which are capable of triggering a new conflict cycle in a particular interpersonal relationship, one may be able to choose the right time and place for the conflict to occur, and temporarily or permanently to control the conflict and its costs.

If one can impose constraints on the way a conflict manifests itself (e.g., by outlawing especially destructive or provocative tactics), one may be able to protect the social system from the more disruptive consequences of the conflict and eliminate the sources of escalation, maybe even achieve some de-escalation.

If one or both principals can develop better methods for coping with the affective consequences of interpersonal conflict, they can function better individually and as a pair even without resolving the issues in dispute. Coping techniques include ventilating one's feelings to friends and obtaining support from them, as well as enlarging one's general tolerance for conflict.

These several control strategies have limitations and involve additional risks. Control strategies that operate by completely avoiding or significantly constraining the form of the manifest conflict may drive the conflict underground, where it becomes less direct but more destructive and more difficult to manage; and/or they may result in an accumulation of unexpressed feelings that will make the manifest conflict, when it does occur, more intense. A further difficulty lies in preventing the ignition of conflict by raising the barriers to expression of conflict: such barriers tend to prevent potentially *constructive* confrontations as well as other tactical interchanges.

CONFRONTATIONS AND STRATEGIC THIRD-PARTY FUNCTIONS

As we just noted, it is possible to handle a conflict merely by allowing the two participants to pursue their own respective strategies of avoidance, constraint, and coping. Therefore, the *direct confrontation* between participants must be treated as an optional step in an overall conflict-management strategy. We regard it as a potentially useful stage toward the resolution or better control of an interpersonal conflict.

If all goes well, confrontations not only allow for the exchange of essential information, but also increase the authenticity of the relationship and the personal integrity experienced in the relationship. If they are not well managed, confrontations can further polarize the individuals, increase the costs of the conflict, or discourage the principals from further efforts to resolve the conflict. One task of conflict management is to maximize the potential gains from a confrontation and to minimize the risks for the participants. The productivity of the confrontation hinges upon many factors with respect to which third-party intervention can perform key functions. We propose that the following are strategic.

1. By his position, the third party often can assess whether the motivation to reduce the conflict is mutual. If there is no sufficient immediate desire on both sides to ensure a give-and-take, the third party can move to avoid or delay the direct confrontation. If there is some positive interest on both sides, but one person has asymmetrically high motivation, then the person with the greater motivation can be encouraged to moderate the level of energy which he invests in the process, pace himself, and structure his expectations about outcomes accordingly. Thus, the third party works to achieve more symmetry in the motivational forces which are activated in the confrontation.

2. An imbalance in situational power will affect the course of the confrontation, by undermining trust and/or inhibiting dialogue between the participants. The third party can attempt to achieve as much balance as possible; for example, by offsetting an organizational power advantage of one, by involving more allies for the other. The third party can regulate the interaction process in a way that favors a person with lesser verbal or fighting skills. Thus, again we propose that the third party attempt to achieve symmetry—this time in terms of the situational power of the two principals.

3. The third party can ensure that one principal's initiative to confront is synchronized with the other's readiness for the dialogue, in order to avoid abortive confrontations. Poorly synchronized confrontations risk heightened feelings of rejection and are marked by a high frequency of misinterpreted acts; for example, a conciliatory gesture may be interpreted as a sign of weakness, or the expression of negative affect by one may be seen by the other as an attempt to perpetuate the conflict rather than as a gesture of trust and an effort to "get it off my chest." To continue the theme of the importance of symmetry, we can conceive of the synchronizing function as a way of achieving symmetrical definitions of the situation by the two parties in conflict.

4. A related function is to ensure either that the differentiation phase of

the dialogue is worked out fully before moving on to the integrative phase, or at least, that a sufficient amount of differentiation has occurred to provide a basis for the amount of integration contemplated for the time being. The underlying principle governing the third party's actions is that, given a conflictful history of the relationship, the potential for genuine integration at any point in time during the confrontation is no greater than the adequacy of the differentiation already achieved.

5. The third party can assess the extent to which various factors contribute to openness in a confrontation; in particular these factors are organizational norms pertaining to expression of differences, emotional reassurance available to participants, and the skills at hand for facilitating dialogue. Depending upon his professional identity as well as his active interventions, the third party may be able to affect the norms of the group and be seen as a potential source of emotional support and process facilitation.

6. The third party can contribute to the reliability of the interpersonal communications: by translating or restating the messages until the sender and receiver agree on the meaning; by procedural devices which require one to demonstrate that he understands what the other has said; and by contributing to the development of a common language with respect to substantive issues, emotional issues, and the dialogue process itself.

7. The third party can attempt to achieve an optimum level of tension in the interpersonal system, sometimes raising the tension level in order to create a sense of urgency and to increase the amount and saliency of the information exchanged; and at other times relaxing a superoptimal level of threat which had begun to produce rigidity in individual thought processes and high distortion in the interpersonal communication processes.

We propose that with regard to the seven ingredients in an interaction setting, none are sufficient and all are necessary in some significant measure for a successful confrontation—that is to say, one in which positive outcomes exceed the costs and any negative outcomes. Moreover, we hypothesize that each of these ingredients is a variable capable of influencing the amount of resolution or improvement in the control of the conflict. If formalized, the hypotheses would take the following illustrative form:

Assuming all other ingredients are present in moderate and adequate amounts, the more symmetrical the situational power of the principals, the more successful will be the confrontation.

The formalization of these hypotheses, which seems unnecessary for the purposes of this book, would merely make more explicit our theory of third-party interventions. By "theory" of third-party interventions, we have in mind both its descriptive and normative applications. As a "descriptive theory" we mean that it postulates relationships between, on the one hand, certain properties of a temporary social-system structure (e.g., situational power), process (e.g., synchronization), tools (language), and affect (tension level), and on the other hand, certain subsequent states of the more permanent social system, in particular the level of conflict in the continuing two-person relationship. As a "normative theory" we mean that it provides a rationale for third-party decisions.

THIRD-PARTY INTERVENTIONS: THE TACTICAL OPPORTUNITIES

If the preceding discussion of functions provides a theory, the discussion of tactics below describes the practice of third-party interventions.

The two discussions necessarily overlap because it is difficult to analyze a function without illustrating the behaviors which perform the function. Similarly, one can't merely list tactical behaviors without some reference to their usefulness. Nevertheless, both functions and tactics need to have their turn at being in the foreground of our analysis of the third-party role.

The simplest and most passive third-party intervention is to be present and available in the confrontation. Depending, of course, on his particular personal and role attributes, the mere presence of a third party in the situation can perform a synchronization function. In addition, his presence can influence the group norms governing openness, can reassure the participants who see him as a source of nonevaluative acceptance and emotional support if needed, and can decrease the perceived risks of failure because he is presumed to possess skills that can facilitate dialogue. The latter three effects serve to increase the participants' willingness to be open in confronting each other.

The more active third-party interventions can be organized under four headings: preliminary interviewing, structuring the context for the confrontation, intervening in the ongoing process, and assisting follow-up activities.

First, preliminary interviews between the third party and the principals are used to assess motivation, obtain other relevant information, promote principals' familiarity and experience with the processes of openness and confrontation, establish appropriate third-party role relationships, and provide all concerned with a better basis for deciding whether to proceed toward a confronting dialogue.

Second, the third party can influence the physical and social context for the confrontation. By choosing a neutral site, one can preserve symmetry in the situational power of participants. By choosing the degree of formality of the setting deliberately, the third party can influence the amount of emphasis on task disagreements versus emotional antagonisms, and the degree of urgency versus relaxedness in the interaction. By arranging for a relatively open-ended time period similarly perceived by both principals and by protecting the confrontation from interruption, the third party can increase the likelihood that the moves of the principals will be reciprocated in the same session and that some natural pacing of differentiation and integration activities will develop. By determining the composition of the confrontation meeting, the third party can control many factors. The inclusion of other persons has various potential effects: increasing the relevant perceptions and insights; increasing the available support for one or both participants; increasing the perceived risk for one or both parties; and increasing the salience of the larger organizational reality in which the two must ultimately work.

Third, the third party can intervene in ways that directly and immediately affect the ongoing dialogue process. Depending upon its context and the particular target for which it is used, each of the tactical interventions listed below may perform any of the strategic functions proposed in Chapter 6. The third party may referee the interaction process in any of a number of respects, terminating a repetitive discussion, providing equal air time for participants, rewarding constructive and punishing destructive behaviors, etc. He may initiate agenda, that is, provide foci for the principals' discussions. He may clarify the participants' views by restating, summarizing, and translating each party's views (both explicit and implicit meanings) as he has heard them. He may encourage an interpersonal feedback process, asking each principal to exchange the perceptions of the other which they have developed over time and to share immediate reactions to the other as they occur during the here-and-now process. He, too, may participate in that process as a giver and receiver of feedback, as appropriate. He may share his own diagnosis or encourage a collaborative effort to develop diagnostic insights. He may prescribe discussion techniques that assist the parties in joining issues and engaging each other more directly, for example, asking a party to provide the historical data of the events on which his feelings toward the other were based. He may diagnose conditions causing poor dialogue, where discussion techniques can't remedy the difficulty (e.g., where indifference or fear is operating to circumscribe the participation of one party). The third party may counsel the participants (e.g., on coping techniques).

Fourth, the third party can assist the principals to plan and prepare for further dialogue after the confrontation meeting. By teaching them what ingredients make a dialogue productive and by identifying for them, in operational form, the techniques and principles that were used effectively in their own immediate experience, the third party can increase the ability of the principals to continue the dialogue on their own. By either being available himself or building a substitute third party into the process, he can provide for continuing third-party participation, if that is desirable. By ensuring that the principals agree upon a specific time and/or purpose for getting together again, the third party increases the likelihood that the conflict-resolution effort will go forward.

THIRD-PARTY ATTRIBUTES

We conclude that the following five role attributes are generally optimum for third-party work as described in this book, and, therefore, can be used for identifying third parties: (1) high professional expertise regarding social processes; (2) low power over fate of principals; (3) high control over confrontation setting and processes; (4) moderate knowledge about the principals, issues, and background factors; (5) neutrality or balance with respect to substantive outcome, personal relationships, and conflict-resolution methodology.

1. The relevance of high professional expertise is obvious in the types of diagnosis, behavioral interventions, and emotional support and reassurance required of the third party. In our attempt to be specific and systematic about role behavior, we do not wish to detract from the subtlety of the phenomenon. That is, although we have focused on the general character-istics of the third party and his overt behaviors, this does not in any way diminish the clinical skill and interpersonal intuition upon which his behavior must be based, and the ingenuity with which his tactical interventions must be conceived if they are to mesh with, yet also influence, the stream of behavior

2. The disadvantage of high power over the fate of the principals derives from the tendency of power to inhibit candid interchanges and induce approval-seeking behavior by participants.

3. The advantage of high control over process is that it allows the third party to take advantages of the tactical opportunities presented by such factors as physical setting, time boundaries, pacing, composition of group, agenda, etc.

4. At least moderate knowledge about the principals, issues and background is usually an advantage because it enhances the third party's credibility with the principals and increases the likelihood that his interventions will be on target.

5. Basic third-party neutrality with respect to the substantive issues, the personal relationships with the principals, and the conflict-resolution methodology facilitates the development of principals' trust toward him.

Although the cases and analysis in the book focus on the interventions of a third party who is a consultant to the organization, the implications of the study are broader. Other persons in the organization can play third-party roles and make many of the interventions analyzed here. The more they possess the role attributes recommended here, the more third-party functions they can perform and the more tactical opportunities they can exploit.